ALPHABETS OF LEADERSHIP
For Young Minds

ALPHABETS OF LEADERSHIP
For Young Minds

ODUNAYO SANYA

Pyxidia House Publishers

ALPHABETS OF LEADERSHIP For Young Minds
Copyright©2019 by Odunayo Sanya.

All rights reserved. No portion of this book may be reproduced, stored in a retrieval system, or transmitted in any form, or by any means - electronic, mechanical, photocopy, recording, scanning, or other without the prior written permission of the author.

Request for information on this title should be addressed to

Odunayo Sanya

Ikoyi, Lagos, Nigeria
Email: odunayosanya@gmail.com
+234 803 200 6607

Library of Congress Cataloging-in-Publication Data

Odunayo Sanya
ALPHABETS OF LEADERSHIP For Young Minds
ISBN-13: 978-1-946530-19-6 (Paperback)
ISBN-10: 1-946530-19-0 (Paperback)
1. Education - Leadership - Nonfiction 1. Title
Library of Congress Control Number: 2019948982

Edited by Winnie Aduayi
Images by Pixbay and Rick Hughes

Published in Dallas Texas by Pyxidia House Publishers. A registered trademark of Pyxidia Concept llc. www.pyxidiahouse.com
info@pyxidiahouse.com

Printed in the United States of America

To Oluwatofarati, AraOluwa, and Opemipo; as you change the narrative and impact your world.

To every young one out there; you are the future and a force for good. I celebrate you as you contribute to making the world a better place by being the best version of yourself.

AKNOWLEDGEMENT

All thanks to God for His grace and the inspiration for this book.

Life is a journey, and you need intentional companions to make the journey worthwhile; to my husband, friend and co-traveller Oladele, thank you for standing with me and believing in me all the time.

To my parents and siblings, thank you for creating the best support system for me.

To my coaches, John C. Maxwell, Paul Martinelli and Robin Sharma, thank you for the great leadership.

To my editor, Winnie Aduayi, and the team at Pyxidia House for the commitment to birth this book; I appreciate you.

CONTENTS

Introduction 9

A: Accomplishment 13

B: Believe 24

C: Courage 34

D: Drive 44

E: Excellence 52

F: Focus 62

G: Growth 70

H: Humility 80

I: Integrity 90

J: Joy 100

K: Kindness 108

L: Language 118

M: Mindtitude 130

N: No 138

O: Original 148

P: Persistence 158

Q: Question 168

R: Responsibility 178

S: Service 190

T: Time 200

U: Urgency 212

V: Value 222

W: Win-Win 234

X: X Factor 246

Y: You 258

Z: Zest 268

INTRODUCTION

If everyone is born with an essentially similar brain, with more or less the same potential for achieving greatness, why is it then that only a limited number of people seem to truly realise their full potential and excel in life? In a practical sense, this is the most important question for every individual to answer.

The future of our nation and the world depends on the next generation of leaders; for the younger generation to realise their full potential as leaders, we must prepare and develop them early. In the lifetime of every individual, there comes a time when one is presented with an opportunity to do something great; more often than not, it never shows up as an opportunity, it comes clothed in challenges. It will be such a tragedy if that moment finds you unprepared or unqualified for the work which would be your turning point. We must understand that the selection process for promoting anyone into a new opportunity in life does not begin the day the opportunity presents itself. No, the 'world of opportunity' begins to evaluate you long before the opportunity is even conceived. Thus, whether or not you know it, decisions about your opportunities in the future are based on how prepared you are today.

Being a mother of three beautiful ladies continually exposes me to the opportunities of nurturing, character and nation-building. As the globe races toward achieving higher levels of development, globalization and digitization, there is an urgent need to leave a piece of ourselves and the principles which govern success, character and significance with the younger generation.

As my first daughter went into high school, I wanted to present her with a journal I had previously written about leadership principles such as faith, love, discipline, God, joy, character, nation-building. The purpose of the journal was to be a go-to whenever she needed encouragement since she had opted for a boarding house. I knew she would miss home; her principles would be challenged, especially in the company of a multitude of diverse children. I know because I am a product of the boarding house system.

Why leadership? You may ask. Why not leadership? I say.

Quite often, leadership is treated as the exclusive preserve of adults and a subject too complex for young minds. If only we know the limitless possibilities, a young mind represents! We tend to associate leadership with positions and age. The highest form of leadership is self-leadership. The ability to lead self is critical for success, significance and transformation. The best gift we can give our young people is to expose them to leadership at a young age (8 – 23). This journey for the young mind is a guided one. They need us *(parents, aunts, uncles, mentors, teachers, and caregivers)* in whatever capacity we may relate with them to model excellence and trust, to mirror faith and inspire purpose in them. Thus, we must preserve trust as we engage with these young minds.

As I advanced in writing the journal, I encountered a lot of parents, adults, and teachers who expressed the yearning for a body of simple day-to-day knowledge that would daily remind people of the need to live a life of impact and how to live it. I wanted many more people to read these nuggets and practice them within their spheres of influence and with the younger generation. Being a member of The John Maxwell Team, the *Global Youth*

Initiative of April 2018 spurred me to begin a series on Social Media – Facebook and LinkedIn, titled *"The A - Z of Leadership for the Young Mind"*. The series enjoyed great followership. I stopped at the alphabet "U" and encouraged my readers to look forward to the book. Today, we have the complete book with bonus pages of Workbook, set to make all the positive difference in every young life and birth the new generation of great leaders.

I discovered from the various feedback I got that several people romanced a secret desire of taking up writing. I believe we are all a bunch of walking stories and our stories, though different, have the same broad themes of faith, discipline, integrity, success, God, career, family, business, health, joy. The good thing is that we can tell our stories, someone is waiting to be inspired by them; our stories carry in them an impact value. With the extra pages of workbook, you can create your own A - Z stories, and who knows, maybe someday publish. You may wish to present them as gifts or bequeath them as compasses to the younger generation, including your children.

This book is not prescriptive. It is to remind you of ALL you know, but due to the pressures of life, may have gotten buried deep in the cemetery of your subconscious mind. It is to spur you as an adult to take responsibility for the younger generation, whose future you are a custodian of. As you read, I hope that you will commit to practising all that is in it, and I hope that it elevates your life and the lives of the young ones around you. The principles in this book can be used to transform communities and nations. Thus, let this book serve as a flame that rekindles your passion for living and leaving a legacy.

A: ACCOMPLISHMENT

"It doesn't matter how great your shoes are if you don't accomplish anything in them."
— Martina Boone

Wale was in elementary school when his dad first encouraged him to take a chance on leadership roles in the school. His dad taught him to work hard, set goals for himself, take his shots and lead. In his first year in high school, his teacher noticed that though he was mostly quiet, he was very motivated with a can-do attitude, and thus, got him signed up on the Literary and Debating team. Wale was sceptical at first, as he was not much of a talker, and thus never thought he had the ability as a public speaker until he went out for the debate at the urging of his dad. With each debate outing, he gained more experience, his confidence grew, and he became the best debater in the school.

In university, he was rejected for a position on the school magazine that he really wanted, to explore his writing skills. That did not discourage him; instead, he went on to start a personal project, a four-page newsletter to compete with the school magazine. Within a few months, Wale's newsletter readership surpassed that of the school magazine. Before the year ended, the school magazine absorbed his newsletter and made him the Editor-In-Chief to lead the magazine in the right direction.

Wale accomplished this great feat and didn't even think of what he was doing as leadership. He only set out to do what needed to be done. He was able to recruit help, and they got it done together. That was his first real leadership role; Wale accomplished something that positively impacted his life and the school community.

This brings us to the leadership alphabet A, which is Accomplishment.

The word accomplish means to finish something successfully or to achieve something *(Cambridge dictionary)*. The key words here are 'finish', 'successfully', 'achieve something' (usually a goal). The dexterity to accomplish is essential for a leader; this is what distinguishes successful people from unsuccessful people.

The ability to nurture an idea into reality regardless of the odds and headwinds encountered is the thin line between success and failure. My father always told me "no one thinks in isolation;" there's always a burst of ideas in the universe. That is the reason why two people with the same idea will present different outcomes: the one who will not take action being fully overcome by fear and the one who will swing into action and change the world with the same idea. To accomplish is to "get it done."

In the words of Colin Powell, *"Leadership is the art of accomplishing more than the science of management says is possible."* He is simply saying you cannot accomplish great feats by being logical, and thus, afraid of the facts that scientific data present to you about your idea, so you have to tackle it head-on; logic will convince you with facts that you cannot get it done."Getting it done" is an important trait of highly successful people. They are the ones who shape the world while others watch. Innate to every human being is the capacity to dream great dreams and do great things. You are capable of much more than you know. Yes, you are human, but you carry in you multiple strengths, unrivalled talents, an unstoppable spirit and willpower. Our purpose is to continually unlock these potentials by letting go of our fears and doing great things.

Myles Munroe described it aptly when he said, "the cemetery is the richest place on earth." Many are buried with their dreams, and they lose the chance to impact humanity. Our youth must understand that talents and gifts are of no value if they are not deployed in the achievement of goals. Fear remains the greatest dread in the attempt to achieve. Fear of what people will say or not say, do or not do, holds us down to the point of paralysis while time continues to pass. This virtue, "Accomplishment," will only thrive in an enabling environment of trust, support and encouragement. We need to encourage the young leaders around us to imbibe the discipline of accomplishment and not remind them of how similar ideas failed before they were even born! We must help them to believe in themselves and their capacity to accomplish.

You may use the example of a race to drive home the point. Only those who FINISH in good time receive medals. Those who finish outside the first to third positions have a story to tell; they finished. Those who stop halfway did not finish; they suffer defeat.

Exercise:

a) Write your stories of accomplishment. Please ensure to keep it simple.

b) What are other things you want to accomplish?

c) How do you plan to accomplish them? Write down your plan. Some changes may be needed as you go along, keep updating and working on your plan.

For me, one of my applications of the A is to encourage my daughter to finish her stories. She writes a lot and has several unfinished stories all over the place.

WORKBOOK

WORKBOOK

WORKBOOK

B:
BELIEVE

"You may succeed if nobody else believes in you. But you will NEVER succeed if you do not believe in yourself"
— John C. Maxwell

Two 10-year-old girls, Ada and Mary, were best friends and both full of energy. Every day after school, the girls would go out playing, racing and chasing each other around in the Estate Recreational Park. They were both very strong and smart girls, but there was a difference. Ada was very optimistic that nothing is impossible and thus, always believed in herself, while Mary ever doubted herself and lived in fear.

One day while they were chasing each other at the

park, Mary missed her step and fell into the pool, and Ada without thinking jumped into the pool excitedly to catch Mary, thinking it was part of the chase game. Both girls did not know how to swim. They struggled in the pool and screamed for help, but there was no help in sight.

After a few minutes of struggle, Mary said to herself, *"I will never get out here alive: I can't swim, neither can Ada, so she can't help me, and I will soon become tired."* Doubting herself and her own survival instinct, Mary did become too tired, gave up struggling and began to sink.

On the other hand, Ada, in her usual optimistic outlook to life, kept on fighting, telling herself, *"No, doubt, it all seems difficult, but I am strong, and I believe I can beat this, so I will keep fighting and somehow I will surely get out of this."*

Believing that she could beat this situation and not drown, Ada kept fighting. Her constant splashing and hand movements attracted the attention of a stranger driving by, who then stopped as he realised what was happening. He ran over and dived into the pool and rescued Ada, who kept coughing and pointing to her friend at the bottom of the pool. The stranger dove back in and pulled out Mary. Thankfully, Mary was still alive but had to spend a few days in the hospital to fully recover.

Ada's staunch belief in herself and her optimism saved both their lives.

This brings us to the leadership alphabet B, which is Believe.

The word believe is defined as "having confidence in the truth, the existence or reliability of something" *(dictionary.com)*. The key words here being 'confidence', 'truth', 'existence', 'reliability', and 'something'. My interpretation of the word is simply to have confidence in the truth of the existence and reliability of ME or YOU. It is important to be a believer in one's limitless capacity to create and achieve set goals. It all begins from the inside.

If you do not believe in yourself, no one will believe in you. Believing in one's self comes with the capacity to love yourself, trust yourself, and accept yourself. Most times, we seek validation outside ourselves. The flip is the case for success; your validations must come from within yourself. Once you believe, the world joins you to believe. Many of us can easily identify with the story of Ada and Mary, albeit, differently.

Sometime ago, I registered for swimming lessons, by

my fourth lesson, my coach took me to the deep side of the pool and asked me to take the plunge. Everyone around cheered and told me I could do it, but this made no difference to me. I only took the plunge when I connected with my belief that I can do it.

As a young leader, it is of utmost necessity that you always believe in yourself; you are only successful to the extent that you believe in yourself. Esteem yourself and your dreams.

The world is replete with examples of people who believed in themselves and changed the course of history. Thomas Edison did not allow his limited education to be a barrier to his dreams; he became a great inventor. Cobhams Asuquo, a renowned Musician and producer, though visually challenged, found ability in disability; so also Nick Vujicic.

The lesson here is to believe in your dream and understand that everything required for the realization of the dream is in the carrier – YOU.

We must encourage our young leaders to see themselves in a positive light. They must let go of the negative beliefs of *"I can't, But, impossible,"* etc. Look at the image of the 'B' leadership alphabet, the cat sees itself as a lion. I assure you the world will soon begin to see it as a lion, not by its physical looks, but by the outcome of its actions. The strength for the Journey of life is in our belief.

Exercise:
Parents, teachers, or any adult can help the young ones with this excercise:

a) Share a story, like the story of David and Goliath, with the young leaders around you to drive home the import of alphabet B: Believe. David, despite his age and inexperience in war, believed that he could take down Goliath and he did!

b) Ask them to hold a mirror to their faces and let them describe what they see in the mirror using positive adjectives.

c) Encourage them to convert "I can't to I can," "I won't to I will."

d) Write what you will do differently if you were Mary.

e) What is your own B? Write what your B is and why.

WORKBOOK

WORKBOOK

WORKBOOK

WORKBOOK

C:
COURAGE

*"Courage is the music that turns
dreams into reality"*
— Aster and Richter Abend

Efe's story started as a young boy. His biggest fear in life was fear itself. Not fear of the dark or real things, but the fear of day to day living; fear of taking a leap, even across a narrow gutter; fear of attempting anything at all because he was always afraid of the "what if." So much fear, he missed out on so many opportunities to excel.

He was also often afraid that he will always feel this way: scared and feeling lonely. It seemed impossible to him that he could ever change, mainly because anxious thoughts were all he had ever known. The older he grew, the more fearful Efe became; he was timid and fretful through elementary and high school, university, and eventually at work, where his fear of fear dealt its hardest blows on him; he was always feeling down about himself and unconfident to deliver his job effectively.

However, one day, Efe had had enough after he was fired from a job he really loved because he lacked the confidence and courage to face his bosses to make a presentation required of him. This really upset him, and thus, made him desire change. He did not know how he would change, but he knew there had to be a way to do that.

Hence, Efe's ultimate fear now became "living the rest of his life in fear," as he realized fear also has a companion called "failure." So, the fear of living in fear became his greatest motivation to change. He told himself that he had just two options: Be depressed forever or work against his fear.

He chose to work against his fear. Living in fear for over 20 years had done enough damage to his life. He was determined, and so he found the courage to face everything he had been afraid to do before, not minding appearing stupid in front of people. He started taking a chance on more productive activities, things that he had always wanted to do, but had been too afraid to do because he was consumed with all the 'what if': what if he fails, what if people call him stupid, what if the shame of getting mocked kills him, and all other what ifs.

Efe found courage by facing his fears head-on. He began making time to learn, develop and hone his skills for the one thing he was always passionate about, Product Marketing, which required him facing people; his biggest fear. It was tough initially, people doubted him and laughed at him, but he found the courage to laugh at himself along with them and worked harder, rather than shrink in fear. He eventually became recognized and respected for his work.

After more than 20 years of living in fear, Efe finally changed his outcome to one of stunning success in his industry when he found courage to make his dreams a reality.

Efe's story brings us to the Leadership alphabet, C, which is Courage.

Gus Lee, in his book titled *'Courage,'* described courage as the "backbone of leadership." I believe the backbone (spine) is what gives frame to the entire human anatomy. The spinal cord makes it possible for the brain to relay messages to different parts of the body to spur action *(study.com)*. Courage is the virtue which makes action possible. Also, William Faulkner puts it so aptly, *"You cannot swim for new horizons until you have the courage to lose sight of the shore."* Faulkner is simply saying here that you cannot hold on to your fears or stay in your safe zone and expect to achieve great heights. Wikipedia goes further to explain Courage - *"it is the choice and willingness to confront uncertainty, fear and pain."* This means courage is from within. Moral courage is the ability to act rightly regardless of the situation.

Every Leader must befriend courage to make phenomenal changes. As a young leader, you must possess the strength to be the lone voice in the desert. Your courage must stem from the conviction that the right things must be done. The societal expectation is that you align with the status quo without question, such that any attempt to be morally upright is often met with various oppositions; this could make your courage immediately morph into fear, if care is not taken. Lack of courage will make you doubt yourself over and over. Courage births the capacity to act. As young leaders, you must keep in mind that as you mature, you will continually have your beliefs and convictions tested by life; the only thing that will keep you moving is your courage. Little wonder Mark Twain said, *"Courage is resistance to fear, mastery of fear, not absence of fear."*

Nelson Mandela, one of the greatest men who ever lived and personified the word courage, described courage so perfectly when he said, *"I learnt that courage was not the absence of fear, but the triumph over it. The brave man is not he who does not feel afraid, but he who conquers that fear."* He believed in his dream to liberate South Africa from apartheid. He stopped at nothing to actualize this. He mortgaged his freedom for 27 years of painful solitude, torture and punishment. Courage and resilience saw him through.

Martin Luther King Jnr., another great leader, did not only dare to dream, but he also had the courage to share his dream of human equality and dignity with millions of people. The dream, no doubt, lives on!

Ever read or heard about the story of David and Goliath in the Bible? That is the story of courage and self-belief.

Here are some pointers to remember:

- The antidote for fear is courage.
- When you practice courage, you master fear.

- Courage is a choice. It is choosing to do the right thing when everyone else is doing otherwise. It is asking the right questions.

- Courage may not make you accepted, but it will make you respected.

Exercise:

Parents, teachers, or any adult can help the younger ones with this excercise:

a) Share more examples of courageous leaders with them.

b) Ask the young leader to write what he or she understands courage to be.

c) Ask for situations in which he or she has exhibited courage. Write it down.

d) Ask for when they found it difficult to show courage. Write it down.

e) Encourage them to always practice courage by self-affirmations like, "I can do this," etc.

WORKBOOK

D: DRIVE

"If you have DISCIPLINE, DRIVE and DETERMINATION... nothing is impossible"
— Dana Linn Bailey

Being crippled did not stop Kgothartso Montjane. She refused to see her condition as a hindrance to living her dream life. She chose to see herself like everyone else; everyone is simply different. She was driven by her dreams to become a Tennis player and to play at the Wimbledon tournament someday.

When no one else could believe in Kgothartso, her determination and drive kept her working hard and training to build up herself strong and ready for the opportunity when it presents itself.

In 2018, Kgothartso finally got her opportunity, and she travelled alone to play her debut Wimbledon tournament. She had to assemble her wheelchair alone; she had no coach with her and no practice partners, unlike her other competitors at the tournament. This was enough to break anyone, but she was driven, and so was blinded to all limitations, there was no stopping her. It was her first time playing on grass; wheelchair can be challenging to move around on the grass. All the odds seemed to be against her, but she was not moved by the odds, she was driven by her goal.

Kgothartso won her debut match at Wimbledon 2018 and became the first black South African woman to compete at Wimbledon. Her drive got her to stardom.

Every journey begins with the first step, and this step leads us to the leadership alphabet D - Drive.

No matter what your journey is, it all begins with drive. Imagine you need to get to an important destination on time, how do you get there? What readily comes to mind is the word "Drive," especially if it is not within close proximity. In the same vein, if you have to get to an important destination in life called Purpose; how do you get there? The answer is Drive! Yes, you drive yourself into your purpose. It is drive that makes a person not accept the status quo, and it is drive that makes someone not to want to be mediocre.

Drive is defined in psychology as "an innate biologically determined urge to attain a goal or satisfy a need". It is also described as "a force that urges or compels (animals or people) to move in a certain direction." The direction, in this case, will be your set goals and objectives. Drive is a verb, and so it implies action, an inner direction of energy from within you which results in an outward movement or realization of a set goal or objective.

It is a natural instinct which operates within the domain of the human mind. It is also referred to as self-motivation. Drive can be connected to from the outside, but its origin is within. It is intangible yet so powerful. It is that fire under your belly, that rises when you need to get things done. Drive is energy. It keeps you going regardless of the situation that surrounds you.

Drive helps with the mastery of fear. Remember that fear is the door you must walk through to access your dreams. Fear cannot withstand the potency of Drive. Drive, just like steam, is lost if action is not immediately taken. A leader's drive is always the rallying point for the team.

Here are some things you can do to build drive:

- Clearly Outline your goals.

- Write or represent in drawing why you must achieve these goals.

- Write or represent in a drawing how you will feel when you achieve the goal.

- Paste the writing or art by your bedside where you see it first thing in the morning and the last thing at night.

- Practice daily positive self-affirmations about having the capacity to deliver on the goal.

<u>Exercise:</u>
a) What drives you? Write it down.

b) Write down how you plan or intend to achieve the dream(s). Drive responds to plans and not wishes.

WORKBOOK

WORKBOOK

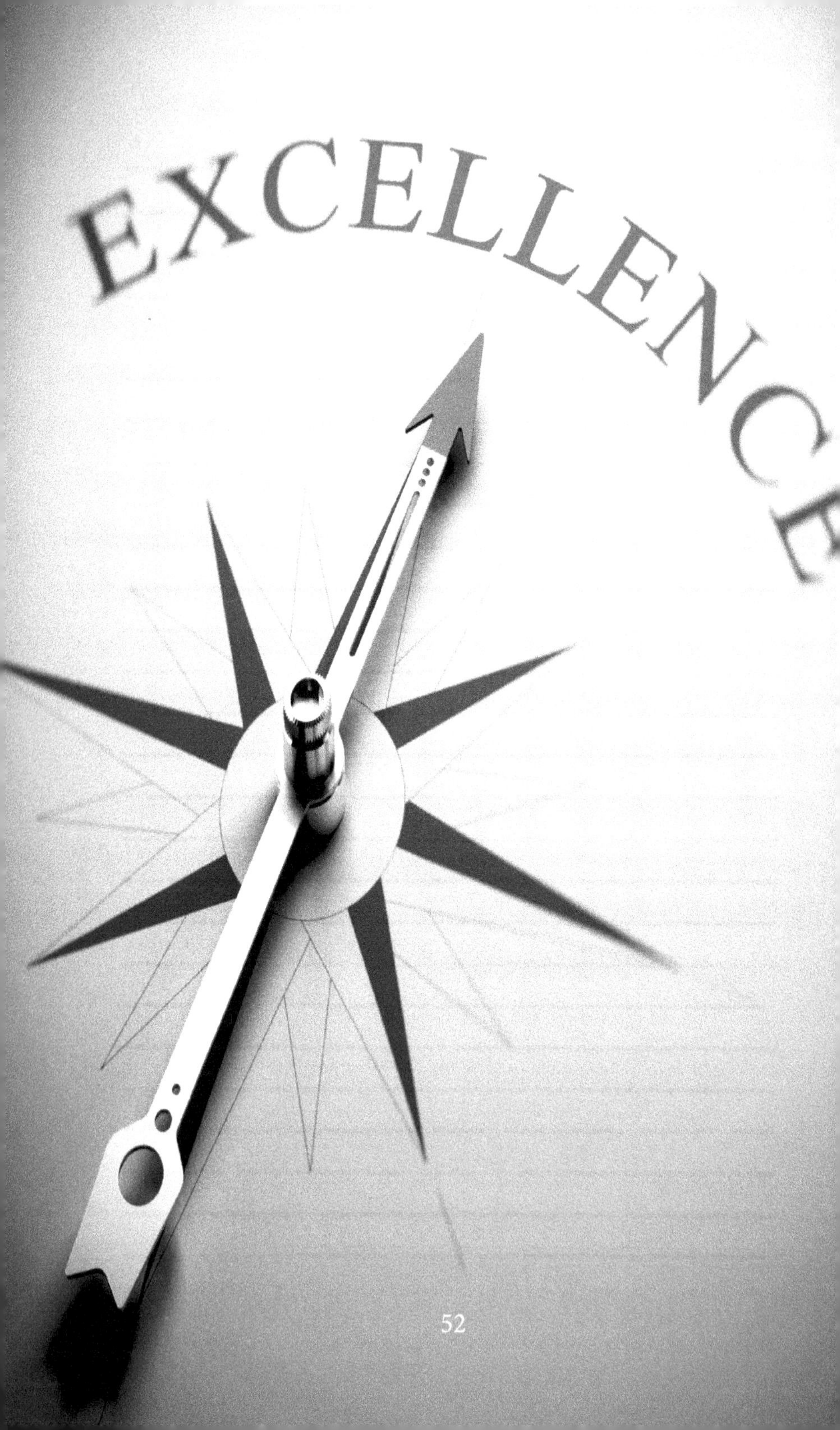
EXCELLENCE

E: EXCELLENCE

"We are what we repeatedly do. Excellence, therefore, is not an act, but a habit"
— Aristotle

Andrew visited his friend, Samuel, who is a Sculptor, where he was sculpting the President at the City Centre, and then Andrew noticed another sculpture exactly like the one Samuel was making lying on the ground next to him. Surprised, he asked Samuel, "Do you need two statues of the same President?"

"No," replied Samuel without looking up, "We need only one, but the first one got damaged when I was to install it."

Andrew examined the image on the ground but did not find any apparent damage. "Where is the damage?" he asked.

"There is a scratch on the nose of the President," Samuel replied, still busy with his work.

"Where are you going to install the President?"

Samuel replied that it would be installed on a pillar 20 feet high.

"If the image is that far up who is going to know that there is a scratch on the nose?" Andrew questioned, looking confused.

Samuel stopped his work, looked up at Andrew, smiled and said, "I will know it, and that's important to me! To be excellent is exclusive of the fact whether someone appreciates it or not. Excellence is a drive from the inside, not outside. It is not for someone else to notice but for your own satisfaction and efficiency. Don't climb a mountain with an intention that the world should see you, climb the mountain with an intention to see the world."

On that note, we arrive at the leadership alphabet E - Excellence.

Excellence is execution to the best of one's ability. It is not to the best of another's ability but the very best of one's ability. Excellence is defined as the quality of being outstanding or extremely good *(google)*. These definitions suggest that we can make a habit of success. Remember, life is a habit; you make out of it what you continually plough into it. Excellence is refusing to be substandard. It is making sure your delivery is 100+ percent all the time, any time and every time. After all, we are the result of what we repeatedly do. As John Maxwell rightly said, *"Leaders don't rise to the pinnacle of success without developing the right set of attitudes and habits; they make every day a masterpiece."*

To make every day a masterpiece is to be consistently excellent in the big and small things in life. I once had a direct supervisor who mastered the art of "seizing the moment." He never treated any task with levity. If he was told he would give a vote of thanks at a function, though seemingly simple, he would rehearse at least three times before the event. Of course, this habit of excellence paid off for him. He became a top influencer within the organization. He made an impression on me, and I began to pay more attention to the way I handled my tasks.

Excellence is a way of life and a daily commitment

to do the best and be the best in all dimensions of life. It is a state of being and so can be learned. Making a habit of excellence entails the following:

- Document your dream(s).
- Plan: Daily, weekly, monthly, yearly.
- Acquire competencies and skills.
- Discipline and accountability.
- Be committed to your dreams.
- Learn to manage your time. Set priorities.
- Have a Positive mindset.
- Build character. Integrity matters.

Excellence will take you places. Employers always look out for this trait in potential employees while reinforcing it in existing employees. Excellence will distinguish you from the others. To make excellence a habit, practice the six points mentioned above on a daily, consistent basis until it becomes a part of you (habit).

Remember, it takes a short while to create a great impression and a lifetime to fix a bad one. Make up your mind to be excellent!

Exercise:
a) Write down your understanding of the word 'excellence.'

b) In what areas of life do you struggle to be excellent?

c) Make a commitment to be excellent today (Write down your commitment, so you never forget)

d) Are there things you need to let go off like; time wasters, unprofitable relationships. Write them down.

WORKBOOK

WORKBOOK

F:
FOCUS

"To Create something exceptional your mindset must be relentlessly focused..."
— Giorgio Armani

Sometime in February 2018, I attended my daughter's inter-house sports ceremony in her school. She looked forward to having her family around as she was participating in over eight events, especially track events. As the day progressed, it was time for the 4 x 100m relay race for girls, and she had tipped her team for gold in this particular race. The shot rang, and the race began, my daughter was on the first 100m lap, and her team (Amber) was far ahead. After the first baton exchange, the team was still ahead. The third baton exchange still saw her team in the lead, then suddenly the team member instead of taking the bend to hand over the baton for the last lap, took a different route.

Unfortunately, this move caused another athlete from a different team (Opal) to lose focus and followed her competition onto the wrong route. The jeers from the crowd dawned a sudden realization, so the Amber team member who led the wrong way quickly retraced her steps and handed the baton to her team member for the final lap. With this singular act, team Amber finished third place with a bronze medal to the team's credit, instead of first place, while Team Opal was not so lucky and finished without any medal to their credit.

The team members learnt a valuable lesson from this incident, that to be successful in life, they must pay attention to the rules of the game and stay focused. They have to keep their focus on the right path and the goal; otherwise, they may miss a good opportunity in life. They understood the importance of consistent focus on what they want and where they are going.

This brings us to the leadership alphabet F – Focus.

To focus is to pay particular attention to someone or something, it is also to adapt to the prevailing level of light and be able to see clearly *(online dictionary)*. Focus is a fundamental attribute in Leadership. To achieve anything in life, one must employ the power of focus. To focus is to bring one's entire being in congruence with set goals. It is to hold the image of your dreams in your mind long enough to create a burning passion and fuel for achievement.

The story above conveys the power of focus. The moment the athlete took her eyes off the goal and intended path to get the gold, she got carried away and cost not only herself but her entire team members the much-desired gold medal.

In life, we often set out with goals in mind, with our dreams, and then we experience distractions which tend to overwhelm us. At this point, there are only two options: Get ourselves back together and refocus or allow ourselves wallow in the sea of distractions while watching our dreams sail away. Focus provides direction.

Distractions may come in the form of:
- Fear.

- Peer pressure: when your friends try to persuade you to ditch your dreams or your values.

- Desire to be like someone else. Stay on your lane and be you.

- Poor prioritization.

- Random negative thoughts.

Focus and lack of focus are both contagious. The story above drives this home. Team Opal was distracted by Team Amber's loss of focus; you know how that ended. Imagine a game of darts; you need to focus because you must keep your eyes on the board to get a good shot.

The more you focus, the clearer your dreams become. Focus!

Exercise:
a) What is your understanding of focus.

b) What makes it difficult for you to focus.

c) Parent, teachers, or any adult help the young ones choose a task to focus on with timelines for monitoring. Write down what the task is and how long you have to complete it successfully.

d) Write a feedback as to the level of focus exhibited during the task.

WORKBOOK

G:
GROW

"In this world, you are either growing or dying, so get in motion and grow"
— Lou Holtz

Ten-year-old Yolanda went to her grandmother's and proudly announced that she was going to be very successful when she grows up and asked if the grandmother can give her any tips on how to achieve this.

The grandmother nodded, and without saying a word, took the girl by the hand and walked her to a nearby plant nursery. There, the two of them chose and purchased two small tree plants. They returned home and planted one of them in the back yard and planted the other tree plant in a pot and kept it indoors. Then her grandmother asked her which of the plants she thinks will be the most successful in the future.

Yolanda thought for a moment and said the indoor tree would be more successful because it's protected and safe, while the one outdoor has to cope with the elements.

Her grandmother shrugged and said, *"We'll see."*

Her grandmother carefully tended to both plants and in a few years, Yolanda, now a teenager, came to visit her again and reminded her grandmother that she never really answered her question from when she was a little girl about how she can become successful when she grows up.

The old woman showed the teenager the indoor tree and then took her outside to have a look at the towering tree outside and asked her, *"Which one is greater?"*

Yolanda replied, *"The outside one. But that doesn't make sense; it had to cope with many more challenges than the one inside."*

The grandmother smiled and said, *"Remember this,*

and you will be successful in whatever you do: ***If you choose the safe option all of your life you will never grow, and when you don't grow you will never be all that you can be. But if you are willing to face the world with all of its challenges, you will learn from those challenges and grow to achieve great heights."***

Therefore, the leadership alphabet G is GROW.

At the beginning of the year 2018, I chose a word which would define everything I do. I chose the word GROW. Over the years, I have learnt that the only way to live a fulfilled life is to GROW in all dimensions of life – spirit, soul and body. Growth must occur in these three dimensions else we begin to feel insufficient and unfulfilled. The single law of existence is GROW. If we are not growing, then definitely, we are dying. Imagine that we remained babies all through life or that when a seed is planted, it remains the same without growing. The mystery of growth is that growth is a choice.

Grow, according to the Merriam Webster Dictionary, is to spring up and develop to maturity, to increase in size and to have an increasing influence. By this definition, it suggests that there is a positive change in the state of anything said to grow – increase, develop. The word 'grow' is a verb, and this means an action is required to achieve it. If you desire to grow, then you must do something about it. I must say at this point that growth is never easy, you have to make sacrifices and adjustments, which is usually worth it at the end.

As a youth, your life is set before you. You have been handed a blank canvas on which to paint the picture of your life. The picture you paint will be exciting to the degree you are willing to grow. Princewill Osaro Omorogiuwa, in his book, *'Achieving the Phenomenal In Africa',* pointedly wrote, "*The powers that a richly developed mind can bring are limitless and within the reach of all who are willing to lend their time to the process of growth.*"

Growth is a journey from where you are to where you want to be. To grow, you must have a clear mental picture of who and what you want to be or achieve. This picture is what you grow to become.

Just as a good seed needs good soil, sunlight, and water to grow, the following are some requirements for personal growth:

- Discipline and Resilience: Be committed to your growth.

- Take responsibility: Your growth is your responsibility.

- Develop yourself intellectually: Enrich your mind with sound knowledge. Pick up a skill, get training, read good books, get educated. Never stop learning; this is the fast track to growth. Education is beyond the four walls of a school; it is a life long learning.

- Questioning: Ask questions.

- Good company: Whom you hang out with determines whether you grow or not.

- Learn from failure: Failure always has something to teach, so pay attention to it and never give up for it. This is very important for growth. *"Every failure carries with it the seed of an equivalent advantage."* – Napoleon Hill.

Exercise:

a) Paint a mental picture of whom you want to see yourself become. (You can write this down).

b) Make an assessment of where you are versus where you want to be – your current picture versus the mental picture. Write it down.

c) What gaps do you see? Is it knowledge, communication, relationship, or responsibility gap? *Please note that it doesn't take a gap to grow! In being the best version of yourself, you move from better to best.

d) Clearly state how you intend to close the identified gaps.

e) Create an actionable plan to move you toward your goal through growth.

WORKBOOK

WORKBOOK

H:
HUMILITY

*"Humility is not thinking less of yourself;
it is thinking of yourself less"*
— Rick Warren

Once, President George Washington was riding near Washington city with a group of friends, and they came to a place where they had to leap over a wall. In the process, one of his friend's horse knocked off a number of the stones from the wall.

President Washington said, "We better replace these stones."

His friends said to him, "Oh no; Mr. President, let the farmer do it."

However, President Washington didn't feel right about that. So, when the riding party was over, he went back the way they came, found the wall and dismounted from his horse. Then he carefully replaced each of the stones.

His riding companion saw what he did and said, "You're too big to do that, Mr. President."

The President's only response was, "On the contrary, I am the right size."

It did not matter to Washington that he was the President of the United States of America and that the farmer was his subject; he humbled himself and showed respect to the farmer by fixing the wall, which his friend's horse broke. Little wonder he was one of America's most exceptional leader: He was a Military General and led Patriot forces to victory in the nation's War for Independence. He was a Statesman and Founding Father of the United States of America, who also served as the first President of the United States. His lifestyle of humility earned him a place in history.

More often than not, we come across similar situations like Washington's, presenting us with the opportunity to be considerate of another, and each time, we see different outcomes with different people.

This brings us to the leadership alphabet H – Humility.

Now, let's imagine a conversation between you and another person, where you emphatically and repeatedly assert your point. The other person tries to state his facts, but you remind him how wrong he is. You are commended for the brilliant delivery of your point, only to discover later that you were very wrong. The twist to this is that no one needs to know you were wrong, and you have the choice to keep it to yourself. The question is, what will you do; will you come forward to say you were wrong and apologise? Or will you, out of pride, rather keep it to yourself and pretend you were right?

Let us consider another scenario where you had to deliver on a project. You insist on a particular method without buy-in from other members of your team. The project fails. What will you do? Will you take responsibility and apologise to the team or will you call their bluff?

Humility is about being modest, respectful and putting others before yourself. It is not calling attention to yourself or being rude and selfish. It is about gratitude and attitude. Better still *Christianbiblereference.org* puts it even more aptly, *"Humility or humbleness is a quality of being courteously respectful of others. Rather than 'me first,' humility allows us to say, 'no, you first, my friend.' Humility is the quality that lets us go more than halfway to meet the needs and demands of others. Acting with humility does not in any way deny our own self-worth. Rather, it affirms the inherent worth of all persons."*

Humility is often misunderstood as having low self-esteem or thinking of one's self as inferior. On the contrary, it is the hallmark of a great leader or achiever, as we see in President Washington's example. Humility is the virtue that enables one to embrace diversity. It is what allows us to see the value in another person. Humility is a perspective that adds value to people.

Humility is not reducing your self-worth; instead, it is being yourself and letting others be themselves without judgement. It enables us to accept feedback, and it gives permission to others to be themselves around us, it engenders complete candour in relationships.

It is pertinent to note that humility is not synonymous with an inferiority complex. Instead, it is the confidence that there is value in you, and likewise in every other person.

Below are some attributes of humble Leaders:

- They listen: Everyone has something to contribute.

- They embrace diversity: Understand that our strengths lie in our differences.

- They do not think lowly of others.

- They are comfortable with the genius of others.

- They admit their shortcomings.

- They are eager to learn; they acknowledge they do not know it all.

As you journey in life, humility will prove a great co-traveller. It will open doors for you and set you among great people.

Exercise:
a) What is your idea of humility?

b) What do you think of President Washington's action, and what would you do if it was you in that situation?

c) On a scale of 1-10, how comfortable are you with

other people expressing their views?
d) On a scale of 1-10, how well do you listen?

d) Practice listening without interrupting.

e) Practice the liberating art of admitting your mistakes.

WORKBOOK

WORKBOOK

I:
INTEGRITY

"One of the truest tests of integrity is its blunt refusal to be compromised"
— Chinua Achebe

James Doty is a man of many talents, which includes neurosurgeon, entrepreneur, and university professor. Early in his career, he was heavily involved in developing the technology and bringing to market the Cyberknife *(the only fully robotic radiation delivery system to treat cancerous and non-cancerous tumours and other targets, precisely delivering radiation anywhere in the body)*. In the process, he became wealthy beyond his wildest dreams.

With a net worth of $75 million, he pledged stock worth $30 million to charity. Not long after the pledge, his investments were struck by the dot. com crash of year 2000 - 2001. Doty lost almost everything. The only thing left was the pledged stock.

His lawyers advised Doty that he did not have to pay the pledge. They told him people would understand that his circumstances had changed and that they wouldn't expect him to follow through on his pledge.

Doty considered his options, and said, *"One of the persistent myths in our society is that money will make you happy. Growing up poor, I thought that money would give me everything I did not have: control, power, love. When I finally had all the money I had ever dreamed of, I discovered that it did not make me happy."*

With the price he had to pay now much higher than he initially thought it would cost him, Doty followed through on his commitment and paid the full pledge; he gave it all. The irony is that only after the gift was given did James Doty find the happiness he had been searching for so long.

James Doty's experience was a daunting one, but his reaction to it is jaw-dropping, and that brings to mind the alphabet I of Leadership, which is

Integrity.

Several corporate organizations and individuals have INTEGRITY as a core value. Integrity is synonymous with honesty, honour, sincerity and virtue. In our various careers, many of us are appraised on the extent to which our behaviour and attitude align with the values of our employer or organization, one of which is integrity. The measurement is usually on a scale of 1 - 4 (one being the lowest and four being the highest). An argument once ensued in my office when an individual scored 3. In my personal opinion, I believe there's no midway with integrity; you either have it, or you don't.

Integrity is the quality of being honest and having strong moral principles that you refuse to compromise. It can also mean someone's standards of doing their job and that person's determination not to lower those standards *(Cambridge dictionary)*. The word integrity evolved from the Latin word 'Integer' which means whole or complete. Wholeness, in this context, is linked to honesty and consistency of character *(Wikipedia)*.

I particularly like the phrase "consistency of character;" my interpretation of which is "Walk the Talk." It is vital that what we say and what we do are aligned. In relationships, whether official, blood, marital, or business, it is key that our actions are consistent. This is what strengthens our character. Integrity breeds trust, candour and accountability. It births high performance in individuals and teams. A Leader must not only exude integrity; he or she must also create a culture of integrity. A culture of integrity is best created when words and actions of leaders are congruent.

Integrity is knowing when to walk away from an opportunity because it is not in alignment with your core values. It is being consistent in character when everyone is watching and when nobody is watching. Integrity always begs the question, if nobody is watching, what will you do?' Will this be different from what you would do if all eyes are on you?

Beyond morality, integrity is delivering 100 percent all the time. It is not delivering 100 percent on Monday and 30 percent on Tuesday – 100 percent ALL the time. It is making sure that the quality of your output is unquestionable and that "your word" is your bond.

Exercise:
a) If you were Doty James, what will you do

differently in this kind of situation, having lost everything, and all you have left is the pledge that you promised?

b) Identify a leader around you who exudes Integrity.

c) Write down the characteristics you most admire in this person.

d) Identify a leader around you whom you think is without Integrity.

e) Write down the character traits that turn you off about this person.

f) Compare your character traits with those of the two leaders you identified, and identify the strengths that you need to reinforce to become better.

g) Create a plan for daily improvement: tangible things to be done. Start implementing your plan from now.

h) Make a pledge to yourself to be a person of integrity.

WORKBOOK

WORKBOOK

J: JOY

"Joy is the holy fire that keeps our purpose warm and our intelligence aglow"
— Hellen Keller

"The secret to personal power and success was sitting right within me all my life, but I just didn't know it," Michael said to Phillip, smiling.

Michael grew up a negative, cynical child, and it wasn't until relative adulthood that he discovered the ability for joy to help him find his power in otherwise powerless situations, especially on his job. Thus, Michael decided to be unconditionally joyful, and he came to understand that it is much simpler than he could ever imagine.

His first step was to stop focusing on what friends, family, colleagues or other people expected and told him that he needed to succeed; he realised he was focusing on the wrong things, which put him under too much pressure, thereby blocking the joy within him. Of course, he knew they meant well, and their opinion is important, but he realised that his own opinion about himself was most important. So, he simply began to focus his mind on what he wanted and everything that made him feel joyful.

As Michael continued with this new joyful attitude, no matter what trouble the day brought, great things started to come into his life with ease. The happier he felt, the more favourable experiences he attracted to himself. He gained confidence in himself, and his time at work became more productive; he began achieving better results, whereas previously, he had been stressed and pressured on the same job. Seeing tangible results, only the habits that felt good became his habit.

Just by being happy and appreciative of what he had, Michael started to get other things he wanted. His personal and professional relationships flourished, he was no longer the cynic, and by feeling good from within, he harmonized with a fulfilling and successful life.

A tremendous power lies within every one of us to attract and move us closer to our desired outcome, if we simply focus inwards and tap into it, rather than focus outward on the negative situations we face.

That power is the leadership Alphabet J: Joy.

The dictionary defines joy as 'the emotion evoked by well-being, success, or good fortune; or by the prospect of possessing what one desire's *(Merriam-Webster.com)*. I particularly like the part which emphasizes the 'prospect of possessing'. This means joy is a force; a positive energy which fuels an individual's passion for achieving. Joy, like everything in life, is a mindset. Xandra Nique's article, "*5 Habits of Joyful People*" (*thoughtcatalog. com*), describes joy as "an inner state which remains unaffected and at peace given any outward situation." Joy is (should be) intrinsic to you, as such is not induced by situations around you.

In the journey of personal leadership or team leadership, which is anchored in your purpose or objectives, a leader needs joy. Joy is that positive mental state that enables you to stay connected to your dream continually. No matter how great your dream is, you need to have inner joy (which radiates on the outside) to actualize it. A grumpy self is easily isolated; people don't want to associate with such a person because they radiate negative energy and are bitter at everyone and everything.

Neuroscience and studies of positive psychology prove that joy is a key driver and precursor of success, with two decades of research backing this up. One reason is that positive feelings, which joy produces, make the brain work better. Positive emotion triggers the release of serotonin and dopamine, which significantly enhances motivation, memory, problem-solving, mental focus and the ability to process multiple concepts simultaneously. So, a positive attitude, born out of a joyful spirit, is proven to help you become more successful as a leader.

Our emotions are tied to our productivity. As a leader of self or teams, productivity is high on your agenda; this means you need to radiate joy, which is a positive emotion that is not dependent on your current situation but your future outcome. Life presents us with a lot of distractions, setbacks and at times very impossible situations; your inner joy is the umbilical cord to your dream. Once severed, it becomes difficult to realize your dream. Joy is a prerequisite for selling your Vision to others. Joy is infectious; if you can't infect others with your enthusiasm, it gets tougher to sell your vision.

Being joyful helps you:
- See the positive in people and situations.
- Celebrate and appreciate the gifts and achievement of others.
- Celebrate Your gifts, knowing that you are unique.
- Add value to others: when you are joyful, you don't shoot down the dreams of others; instead, you compliment and encourage them to achieve their dreams.
- Raise your productivity level.
- Rally support for your dream.

As you go through life, make joy your companion.

Exercise:

a) Imagine yourself in a joyful state.

b) What prevents you from constantly living that joyful mindset?

c) Make a plan to eliminate those hindrances.

d) Write out a self-affirmation commitment to be Joyful.

WORKBOOK

WORKBOOK

K:
KINDNESS

> *"Be kind whenever possible. It is always possible."*
> — Dalai Lama

Sarah is hardworking and often delivers her work on time. She has been with the company for seven years. One day, Sarah's boss, Mark, got frustrated with her because she couldn't move as fast as he wanted, and he pulled her into his office and unleashed five minutes of verbal abuse before he fired her. She ran out in tears.

"That felt so good," he said proudly to his business partner, with a big smile.

Mark viewed this incident as a success, but his business partner, Israel, saw this as evidence that Mark was kind to people only as long as they did exactly what he asked or wanted. Otherwise, he cared not one bit about them.

Israel went on to tell Mark that his unkind behaviour is a sign of weakness, not strength, and so he need not be proud of his actions. Pointing out that strong people don't lose control when they don't get their way. Israel went on to share with him that people's kindness makes all the difference in our ability as humans to push through roadblocks, survive setbacks and go over and beyond the call of duty.

"With an unkind spirit, your vision narrows, and you become dangerously impulsive. Being unkind is a deadly flaw for us as leaders because leaders are meant to build; not tear down." Israel said, leaving Mark utterly embarrassed about his action.

This brings us to our leadership alphabet K: Kindness.

I hear you say, "kindness? That's too simple." Indeed, it's simple yet so challenging to attain. This has been reinforced over and over again in school, Sunday school, at home and everywhere. Why then is it that humanity has never really internalized the virtue called kindness?

Sometime last year, I visited the Homeless Girls' Center in Lagos, with my colleagues, where I met a well-spoken young lady named Mercy. Her mom is late, and she had to move in with her sailor dad and stepmother. On one of the days when her father was absent, her stepmom gave her transport money and instructed her to leave the house and never come back. I wonder what the father would have been told when he returned. Most likely it's the usual "she ran away" story. She ended up in the home set up for loitering and homeless children. Mercy would like to become a Doctor in future so she can save lives. A little bit of kindness from her stepmom could have made her journey less traumatic.

As leaders, we must learn to be intentionally kind in our daily living, because the positive attitude necessary to excel in life comes far more easily to people who are intentionally kind. Luis Benitez, who has summited the Seven Summits 32 times, *(the tallest mountains on each continent)*, told the world that kindness and compassion are essential elements to overcome the horrible physical and mental challenges he encounters while climbing. This virtue produces an uncanny "good feeling" within you that strengthens you to keep going.

For example, if you see someone limping on a day when you have to get up to the next camp, you can curse their weakness and ignore their pain, or you can stop for 10 minutes and bandage their feet so they can keep up with you for the rest of the climb. When you finally summit, you do so more fulfilled knowing you gave someone a chance to also summit. Besides, except in a lose or win competitive situations, stopping to help a colleague is one of the fastest ways to ensure you achieve your goals.

Furthermore, by reaching out and being kind to other people, you strengthen your social connections. The stronger your social connections, as a leader, the higher your chances of getting to the peak of success. Strong social connections don't come from constantly asking people favours or manipulating them to get what you want. They come from being genuinely interested in other people, and from having an authentic interest in their well-being. It comes from being willing to help others. It comes from giving of yourself.

Kindness is indeed a virtue, which we must all embrace regardless of ethnic colourations, language, background, religious affinities and doctrines. It is being mindful of the other person, not taking the other person for granted, accepting the diversity of life and mankind. It is adding value to others, not eroding value. Kindness is that virtue which enables sharing as a new system of life, based on the fact that the sharer is committed to improving the livelihood of others. Kindness is deliberately seeing the good that surrounds us and committing to preserving same. Showing kindness is not rocket science, neither is it an endless algorithm. It is a commitment to uplifting others. Simply put, it is the 'Golden rule' – do unto others as you want to be done unto you.

As a leader of self and others, you cannot wish away kindness. You must be kind in your thoughts, words and your actions. Your thoughts will influence your words and actions. Be kind and positive in your thoughts toward others. Your words are important; they can make or break – be kind with them. Speak the truth in love; let your words inspire strength and greatness in others, not otherwise. Your actions are equally important, share a smile, give a pat on the back, a hug, and all kind gestures. Do not hold back from offering a helping hand; not because you expect a reward, but because you choose to pay it forward.

Make no mistake about it, kindness does NOT equal weakness. Quite the contrary. It takes tremendous strength to be kind to someone who is slowing you down or who thinks differently than you do. But kindness bridges such gaps and brings out the talent hidden in so many people. It is a virtue that breeds loyalty and trust.

Mother Theresa crowns it all by saying, *"Three things in human life are important: The first is to be Kind. The second is to be Kind. The third is to be Kind."* Over and over again, the world can benefit from consistent acts of kindness. Make a commitment to be Kind today.

Exercise:

a) Review your thoughts, words, and your actions. Write down some of the words you speak and some things you do for or to people.

b) Describe an incident when someone was not kind to you and how you felt.

c) Assess yourself on a scale of 1-10. Are you kind?

d) In what ways do you think you can be kind? List at least 10.

e) Draw up a weekly plan on how to actualize at least 3 out of the 10 each week.

WORKBOOK

WORKBOOK

L: LANGUAGE

"Words have Power. Use the language of leadership versus the vocabulary of a victim."
— Robin Sharma

Mr. Henderson started teaching his son, Thomas, the power of language at a very young age. Mr. Henderson would always tell his son that certain words affect a person's mental picture and that words are a powerful programming factor in lifelong success.

As a child, Thomas was always climbing trees, and literally hanging around upside down on anything high that he could climb. So, it was no surprise for his dad to find him at the top of a 25-foot tree swinging back and forth. His little seven-year-old brain didn't realize the tree could break or that he could get hurt. He just thought it was fun to be up so high.

Thomas' cousin, Henry, who is about the same age, was also on the same tree. He was hanging on the first big branch that was about five feet below Thomas. Suddenly, a huge gust of wind came over the tree, and the tree began to sway. Thomas dad and Henry's dad soon realized the danger their sons were in.

Thomas' dad yelled, *"Tom, hold on tightly."* So, he did.

The next thing they knew, Henry was screaming at the top of his lungs, lying flat on the ground. He had fallen out of the tree. Thomas scampered down the tree to safety.

Thomas dad later told him why Henry fell and why he did not, even though he was higher up on a slimmer branch. Apparently, when Henry's dad felt the gust of wind, he yelled out, *"Henry, don't fall!"* But Henry fell.

Thomas dad explained to him that the mind has difficulty processing a negative image. That, in fact, people who rely on mental images cannot see a negative at all. Hence, for Henry to process the command of *"don't fall"*, his seven-year-old brain first had to imagine "fall", then try to tell the brain not to do what it just imagined, which is quite difficult. Whereas, Thomas seven-year-old brain instantly had a mental image of himself hanging on tightly.

"You cannot visualize 'not doing something'. The only way to accurately visualize not doing something is to find the right positive 'word' for what you want to do and visualize that instead," Mr. Henderson added.

The words we speak, not just the words we hear, also affect us. Here is a different example of how the words we speak affects us: Rob was a great child and a bit introverted growing up, and no doubt, quite enthusiastic about his future. He had great dreams to change the world, though not quite sure how. As he advanced in age, no thanks to external influences, his language soon began to reflect the everyday lingo of "I can't", "it's beyond my reach", "it's impossible". As Rob's language got re-conditioned, his dreams shrunk, and eventually his outcomes in life were negatively impacted.

This brings us to explore the leadership alphabet L,

which is Language.

Language, according to the dictionary *(google)*, is the method of human communication, either spoken or written, consisting of the use of words in a structured and conventional way. It fuels communication, which is key to Leadership. It enables you to put your thoughts together in a way that is understandable and actionable by yourself and the next person. Usually, our language is a reflection of our experiences, whether good or bad. That is why some people radiate positive energy while some radiate negative energy. I'm sure we all want positive people around us.

Your language will, to a large extent, coupled with action, determine your outcome in life – personal or otherwise. Our dream or vision is meant to be created. Creation starts in the mind with words and pictures. Self-limiting beliefs are the result of learned negative language influenced by other people's self-inflicted complex. These beliefs keep us and our dreams in a state of inertia while life passes by. On the other hand, self-accelerating beliefs are also a function of learned positive language inspired by a great sense of self-esteem and motivated people around you.

"Your Language is the direct translation of your thoughts. Language is powerful. You cannot think

or act beyond the language of your mind."
- Odunayo Sanya.

Here is a simple demonstration of the power of wrong vocabulary. Ask a child to hold a pen. Hand him or her the pen. Now, say these exact words to the child, *"Ok, try to drop the pen."* Then observe what he or she does.

Most people release their hands and watch the pen drop to the floor.

Then you respond, *"You weren't paying attention. I said 'TRY to drop the pen, not drop the pen'. Now, please do it again."*

Most people then pick up the pen and appear to be in some sort of struggle while their hand tries but fails to drop the pen.

The point is made. If you tell yourself you will "give it a TRY," you are actually telling yourself to fail because your mind cannot visualize "TRY"; therefore, it will only visualize the pen "dropping". If you "TRY" and do something, your unconscious mind has permission not to succeed. So, your language plays a critical role in determining your outcome in life.

As a Leader, your language matters. What language

do you think or speak in? Does your language create value or erode value? The language of a leader is that of kindness, truth, respect, faith, success, possibilities, and inspiration. Your language should inspire self-worth and spur your dreams or your team to action. Nurture your dreams with your words, don't stop there, complement it with actions, and you would soon see your dreams grow. Language is a powerful tool in the kit box of a leader.

Language is an enabler of purpose, dreams and vision. Make a commitment to enable yourself and those around you with your words. The good thing about Language is that it is learned and so can be unlearned.

Exercise:
a) Take time to audit your vocabulary. Make a list of the words you mostly use in daily conversations with yourself and others.

b) Write your observation: Are they more of positives or negatives?

c) If negative, make a deliberate effort to convert

them using the opposites. Start by creating a "NEGATIVE and POSITIVE" table in your workbook and write a list of your negative words under the NEGATIVE side of the table, and then write the positive word for each negative word under the POSITIVE table. For example:

NEGATIVE		POSITIVE
1.	Can't	Can
2.	Difficult	Easy

d) Practice self-accelerating beliefs and practice speaking these positive words daily.

WORKBOOK

WORKBOOK

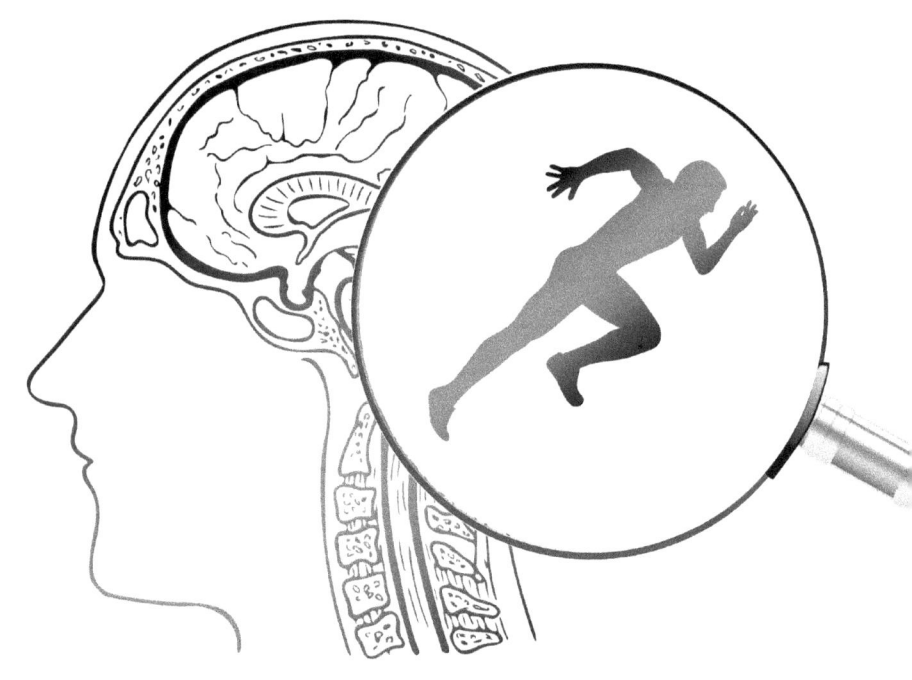

M:
MINDTITUDE

"Your mindtitude determines your attitude."
— Odunayo Sanya

"We may imagine that thought can be kept secret, but it cannot; it rapidly crystallizes into habit and habit solidifies into circumstance. All that we achieve and all that we fail to achieve is the direct result of our own thoughts... As a man thinks, so he is; as he continues to think, so he remains"
— James Allen.

At the end of the nineteenth century, just as colonial Africa was opening up as a market, all the manufacturers of shoes in Britain sent their representatives to Africa to see if there might be an opportunity in Africa for the shoes. All the representatives duly came back in time with the same answer.

"Nobody in Africa wears shoes. So, there is no market for our products there."

However, the Bata representative came back saying, *"Nobody in Africa wears shoes. So, there's a huge market for our products in Africa!"*

After that, Billboards promoting Bata appeared all over Africa, even in the remotest of spots. That's why and how Bata shoes became known as the shoes of Africa.

Did all these people visit the same Africa as the Bata representative? Of course, they did. Each had seen the same things but had viewed and reported differently, because the attitude their minds had developed before even seeing Africa had already taken precedence, and thus, reflected in their outward sense of judgement and conclusions.

The story of Bata shows how our minds have been cultured to process and see things, and how we accept them, either consciously or unconsciously. We encounter so many situations in our daily life, which certainly can make or mar us as individuals if we do not consciously manage the attitude of our minds. How often have you found yourself during a conversation with someone that you already have your response as the person is still speaking to you, without really understanding what is being conveyed to you? Because your mind already decided what your answer will be before the person even finished. Make no mistake about it, the attitude you exhibit outwardly first presents itself in your mind. So, yes, our minds have attitudes that power the course of our lives; the mind is the battlefield for all future success, and your only weapon is the attitude you allow in there.

Hence, this leads us to the word, "Mindtitude', which represents the leadership alphabet M.

What word is that? Well, I took the liberty of coining this word, and so I have the honour of defining it. The etymology of this word is from Mind and attitude. Thus, I will define Mindtitude as the state of mind at any point in time. State, as used here, encompasses health, words, thoughts and disposition. Your Mindtitude is very critical to your success in life. Every action, good or bad, has its origin in a thought. Our thoughts are seeds that grow into action and then shape our reality. Many have lost great life opportunities because of the attitude of their minds. This is why our mind's attitude to looking at things is a quality that must be well-manicured, or it would lead us down the wrong path.

The mind is where life is first lived. The mind is a gift to us; it can be likened to a staging area or a holding bay where we live out our dreams through words and imagery. The created picture is then etched in our memory, this picture becomes our purpose, and all our actions are then aligned to the achievement of this purpose. It is a blank canvas given at creation. What have you made of it?

What is the state of your mind? This is a question we must always ask ourselves. The state of our minds determines our outcomes in life. Fill your mind with great things that inspire possibilities. Never let fear or doubt make your mind a place of habitation. In my journey through life, I have come across bright minds who gave up great dreams because of doubt and fear. You have been resourced with all that you need. Move toward your dreams, put plans in place to make manifest that picture of greatness in your mind. Men are first great in their minds before they are called great. Believe in yourself and never let anyone or you put you down. As James Allen rightly put it, "The human mind may be likened to a garden, which may be intelligently cultivated or allowed to run wild. But whether cultivated or neglected, it must and will bring forth."

Regardless of where you are now, begin to tend to the garden of your mind. Weed out every undesirable thought from the root. Beautify your garden with fresh flowers in the form of positive thoughts, read books that inspire greatness and practice self-affirmations. Take good care of your mind; it is your tool for a fulfilled life. A transformed mind is a transformed life.

Exercise:

Put your mind to work by taking the time to think out great ideas. You can do this by adopting the process below:

a) Step 1: Make a clear mental image.

b) Step 2: Hold it in your thought (Hold your Image).

c) Step 3: Visualize it. See it. Believe it. (You can write a description or draw the image).

d) Step 4: Believe that the *"ways and means of satisfying the desire will follow."* - Robert Collier, *'The Secret of the Ages'*.

WORKBOOK

N:
NO

"The art of leadership is saying no, not saying yes. It is very easy to say yes"
— Tony Blair.

In his teen years, Seyi discovered how quickly saying "yes" would turn people that didn't even like him into "friends". So, it got to a point in his life where his only response was a "yes," as it made him "look good" in the eyes of others. He felt good about earning the reputation of someone that was always willing to put others and what they needed as a priority over himself, regardless of whether his "yes" was also him telling himself "no". He sacrificed much because he wanted people to like him, by saying yes to everyone.

Seyi thought this made him a "good" person; he thought this would gain him the admiration of the people that would have otherwise thought less of him unless he was willing to forgo his own plans with a "yes" to them.

It took Seyi discovering his purpose and understanding that he needed to develop an unbroken focus, if he must fulfil his purpose, to turn his "yes" into a "no."

The day he discovered the word "no" he discovered fire. Seyi learned that a simple "no" had power, and that saying "no" is a self-sufficient act. He learned that to say "no" means to rely on himself and be accountable; it means to overtake any obstacle or distraction that stood in the way of his being victorious in the battle for his own headspace and creativity.

Seyi gave himself no other option but to be successful, by sidelining any distractions or anything that would not further his course, by simply saying "no". With that one single two-letter word, Seyi was able to move mountains and completely recreate the world he was living in.

This brings us to the leadership alphabet N - No.

A favourite word used by toddlers and children of pre-school age is the word 'No.' I remember my children at the same age; even when they had nothing in their hand, and you asked them to give you nothing, they still said 'no.' Reading through many articles, the word 'no' enables these toddlers to assert and protect themselves. I have also observed that as they grow, they become a bit more agreeable using the word 'yes.' Amazingly, we spend time as parents trying to teach a child to become more agreeable only for them to spend their adult years trying to say 'no' to distractions.

The most successful people are good at staying focused, and although there may be people that are more talented than they are, they excel because they have this ability to maintain their laser-like focus by saying "no". When it comes to saying no, the late CEO of Apple, Steve Jobs, was a master. He was one of the few people who would say no to the good things so that he could focus on something great. This is the underlying philosophy that led to Apple becoming one of the greatest companies in the world, creating some of the most technically sound products ever.

No is one of the shortest words in our vocabulary, and also one of the shortest sentences in the English language. It is equally, if not more powerful than the word 'yes'. Most times, our thinking is boxed into opposites which leads us to see 'yes' as positive and 'no' as negative. In the article *"The Power of No"* published on *Psychologytoday.com*, Judith Sills wrote that *"No is an instrument of integrity and a shield against exploitation. It often takes courage to say, and it is hard to receive. But setting limits sets us free."*

No is how you break away from conformity and the need to be accepted. You cannot be a leader if the need to be accepted is more important to you. Robert Siegel, in his article in Forbes Magazine (2014) wrote, *"One of the most useful tools a person has is to say no to things that are taking up time but are not adding much value to one's life."*

If you are to succeed in life, you can't be shy to say No. It enables you to affirm all that you are and stand for. It reinforces your values when tested. It empowers you to move forward toward your goals and objectives. It de-clutters your vision. It is an important tool for attaining self-discipline and accountability. You say no in two ways – internally and externally. Saying no internally is telling it to yourself when you find yourself straying from your commitment. For instance, you desire to lose weight, and you are committed to staying off confectioneries. Then your friend orders some cheesecake; it will take saying a strong 'no' to yourself to keep your commitment. Saying no is when you refuse to be influenced negatively by others. In the course of my career, I have had to say no repeatedly to offers and meetings which are not aligned to my productivity. But for some, it's a different story. For instance, let's look at Ola's predicament.

Ola promised to drive three of his friends in his car to various places on the same day. This happened to be the same day he planned to write the first chapter of his (bestselling) book. What do you think the outcome was? Your guess is as good as mine. Ola disappointed one of his friends because of the heavy traffic, made two of his friends happy but did not get to write the first chapter of his book. What do you think the outcome would have been if Ola aligned his priority to his goals?

Some of the reasons you must say 'No' are:
• It helps with proper time management: your time is committed to executing important goals that are critical to your success.

• It helps you balance the various aspects of your life such that you have time for family, career, leisure and health.

• It keeps you focused on your goal.

- It prevents burnout.
- It keeps peer pressure at bay.
- It enables you to take responsibility for your life.
- It preserves your integrity and relationships.
- It is your right.

When you say 'No' in good time it enables freedom; others can move on with their lives, so can you. Had Ola said a timely 'no' his disappointed friends would have made other arrangements and he would have written the first chapter of his book. As Warren Buffet puts it, *"The difference between successful people and very successful people is that very successful people say 'no' to almost everything."*

Saying 'no' is an art by itself. The way it is said is as important as saying it. How do you say no?

- Try not to be forceful about it except the situation is threatening.

- Don't leave the recipient stranded. Present possible alternatives.

- Be calm, don't say it with burden guilt; this opens you up for manipulation.

Exercise:

a) Practice saying no to requests and activities that do not prioritize your goals.

b) Make a list of some of the times you think you should say no to some requests, stating what these requests are. And write why you think you should say no to these requests. Example:

Time: *When I'm working on my my homework and my friend invites me to play or watch football with him or her.*

Why: *I have not finished my howmework, which is more important than playing or watching football with my friend.*

WORKBOOK

O:
ORIGINAL

"When you are original (authentic), you create a certain energy; people want to be around you because you are unique"
— Andie MacDowell.

Early in her career, Oprah Winfrey was an evening news reporter at Baltimore network, WJZ-TV. But she found it hard to emotionally detach herself from the subjects of her stories and was soon fired from the news beat, for being authentic.

However, upon firing her, the network needed to pay her the remainder of her contract, so rather than pay her that, the network moved her to daytime TV. The rest is history. As a Talk Show host,

Oprah could finally be her authentic self, and her originality became an asset and the key to unlocking her success as an entrepreneur.

"I had no idea that being your authentic self could make me as rich as I've become," Oprah said.

Oprah runs her business and leads her team as authentically as possible. She would always say it wasn't easy because being original is as much about revealing your flaws as playing to your strengths. And that it's often tempting to put up a front of total competence rather than risk looking vulnerable, but she remained true to herself, knowing without a doubt that originality is a key ingredient in running a successful business and leading a great team.

This leads us to the leadership alphabet O: Original.

Recently, I took time out to go to the open market. There were thousands of humans milling around looking for what to buy, but most importantly, at the right price. I noticed a trader and his customer, both actively gesticulating. Then I heard the famous phrase in pidgin English, *"this one na original"* meaning "this is original." Where I come from, the word original is used to describe an unadulterated or unalloyed state. It is often used to convey the qualitative nature of something. The trader was simply trying to convince the customer that his wares are of high standards.

Authentic is another synonym for original. To be original is to be genuine; it is to be yourself. Imagine that everyone in the world looks the same, talks the same and thinks the same, I bet the universe will be boring, and we would miss the great minds that have shaped our world. You are unique and must preserve your uniqueness.

Being original is being comfortable with who you are. Do you love the individual you see when you stare into the mirror? Self-love is at the core of being original. The first rule of a fulfilled life is being comfortable with yourself, your gifts and your talents. I discovered that several individuals wish they were someone else, they believe others are more gifted and thus, wish that other people's dreams were theirs. The truth is, the more you dwell on being someone else, the more you diminish the possibilities of actualizing your own dreams and the more unfulfilled you are.

The concept of being original is brought to life in the movie *'The Greatest Showman,'* played by Hugh Jackman. It is the 'grass to grace' story of P.T Barnum. A man who identified originality as the key to personal and business Success. The acts in his Circus were unique by creation as such were not accepted by the larger society. He helped them see their uniqueness as a strength rather than a weakness. The Circus was quite resilient and successful.

Have you ever stopped to think that the reason you desire to trade places with someone else is because they have worked on their dreams, put their talents to test and believed they are an 'original' not a duplicate or fake? Put your dream, talents and gifts to the test of action and passion; then you would see them bloom like roses.

I remember growing up (age 7-8) and thinking my name was strange. For a long time, I knew only one person with my name. You see, I wanted the more available names, instead of appreciating the uniqueness of my name. Then one day, I summoned the courage and asked my dad why I was named Odunayo. In answering, he told me one of the greatest stories of purpose I ever heard. After that, I decided to own my name, ODUNAYO, which means the year of joy.

"Never desire the common, create the unique. Great legacies and stories abound in uniqueness."
– Odunayo Sanya.

What are you struggling with? In what ways have you surrendered your dream only to admire the dreams of others? What battles of 'not-good-enough' are you fighting? You are the only original version of yourself; you have a right to succeed (only if you work at it). Don't waste YOU; there will never be anyone who can be YOU. Every time I have the chance, I reiterate this, *"it is expensive to be someone else but affordable to be yourself. You have been resourced with all it takes to be you."*

Unleash the greatness in you. Be original!

Exercise:
Parents, teachers, or any adult can help the young ones with this excercise:

a) Start appreciating yourself, stop complaining.

b) Write down the great and unique things about you; celebrate your originality.

c) Encourage your inner self; practice being comfortable with yourself.

d) Write down the things about you that you often

find yourself comparing with other people. Example: "I wish I am as smart as that girl, I will become a doctor."

e) Now, watch to see the things you don't want about that same person. Write these down; then compare your answers in Excercise d with Excercise e.
(See how unique you are when logically compared to that person. She may be smart in the ways that you're looking at, but you could be smarter in other ways that you're just not realising, and still become what you want to be if you apply yourself diligently).

e) Gradually slow down on comparing yourself to others.

e) Set out a plan for realizing your dreams, staying original.

WORKBOOK

P:
PERSISTENCE

"A river cuts through rock, not because of its power, but because of its persistence"
— James N. Watkins.

In his book, *'Think and Grow Rich'*, Napoleon Hill shares the intriguing story of Fannie Hurst.

Fannie arrived in New York in 1915 with hopes of earning a good living using her writing skills. Four years passed and still no breakthrough. She refused to yield to the beats of defeat as would have been perfectly conducted by Broadway.

Then came the moment of victory, the moment for which she had lived and was willing to die.

After 36 rejections from the same publisher, the ice broke, she got her story through. As documented by Hill, *"the moving picture rights to her novel, 'Great Laughter' brought in $100,000.00. This is said to be the highest price ever paid for a story before publication."* Fannie persisted; she was not deterred by the obstacles of rejection that lined her path.

Fannie was able to hold on and keep going after several rejections because her self-will aligned with her desire for success, which produced in her the purest form of persistence.

Thus, the leadership alphabet P is Persistence.

Persistence is foundational for success in life. Every story of success is a story of persistence. It is not giving up in the face of opposition and difficulties. It is possible that the best songs are yet to be recorded and the best books yet to be written, but what we do know is that the published artists and authors were persistent enough to fulfil their dreams and aspirations; they had the end in mind.

Life will present us with many obstacles and hurdles which may leave us disillusioned; it is important that we respond with persistence. The truth is that life tests us with these distractions with a promise of success to those who do not give up; that is life's configuration. We can only achieve our dreams through persistence by learning from our mistakes and converting our failures to growth lessons. How many of your dreams have you given up because you felt the obstacles were too tough? How many times have you killed your ideas because you felt it required too much hard work?

Ask yourself, if you were Thomas Edison, would we have the light bulb today? Edison made 1,000 (one thousand) attempts before he succeeded with the light bulb.

A few years ago, I recall applying and attending interviews for a position in my organization three times before finally getting the job. My first attempt was in 2009, it was a brilliant outing, but things took a sour turn. My second attempt was in 2012, and the third attempt was in 2014, after which I landed the job. I refused to give up; I told myself repeatedly that I had a right to that job. I received job offers from other organizations while waiting for this particular job, and I declined the offers because they did not align with my aspirations. I used my waiting time to train myself and upgrade my skills. The wait time was spent preparing and operating at the next level, and when the time of practice finally came, I was ready.

Reaching higher altitudes in life is not the exclusive domain of a privileged few, but the earned domain of the defiantly persistent. It is not rocket science, a persistent attitude can be cultivated. Napoleon Hill puts it simply, *"persistence is a state of mind and can be cultivated."*

According to Napoleon Hill (2003 *'Think and Grow Rich'* 9:182-183), some symptoms of lack of Persistence include:
- Procrastination.

- Inertia.

- Fear of failure.

- Lack of clarity of purpose.

- Willingness to quit in the face of defeat.

- Wishing instead of willing.

To develop persistence, Hill (2003 *'think and grow rich'* 9:187) recommends:
- A clear purpose backed by a desire for its fulfilment.

- A definite plan expressed in continuous action, and (I add) time.

- A set mind closed against discouraging influences.

- A great inner circle made up of people who will encourage you to follow through on your plans.

It's time to put yourself together and work on your dreams. The fact that someone attained success is a clear indicator that success is also within your reach. Develop persistence, pen down your purpose, create a plan and begin your journey to success today. Your dreams are achievable if only you are willing to pay the price. We are built to persist.

Remember:
Self-will + Desire = Persistence.

Exercise:
Practice persistence:

a) Identify one area in your life where you desire or need persistence.

b) Put together a plan that helps you build persistence.

c) Engage an accountability partner (e.g siblings, parents, etc.) to help keep you on track.

d) Practice persistence in all that you do; never give up.

****

BONUS WORD

A bonus word for leadership alphabet P is Problem-Solving.

Problem-solving is a skill that remains relevant regardless of time. The ability to solve problems separates Great people from Ordinary people. The greatest minds of our time – Edison, Ford, Mandela, Steve Jobs, etc., solved big problems. They created solutions, which elevated and are still elevating the standards of human existence. Humans are social beings, and as such, we are expected to create solutions for the problem of our collective – the family, community or nation.

Have you ever asked yourself why businesses thrive? It is because they solve problems. They create products and services that meet the needs of the consumer without which they would cease to exist.

*What problem are you solving?

WORKBOOK

Q: QUESTIONING

"Learn from yesterday, live for today, hope for tomorrow. The important thing is not to stop questioning"
— Albert Einstein.

Eric Schmidt, CEO of Google, said, *"We run this company on questions, not answers."* He knows that if you keep asking questions you will keep finding better answers and more creative ways to serve the world better.

When Greg Dyke became Director-General of the BBC in 2000, he went to every major location and assembled the staff. They came expecting a long presentation. He simply sat down with them and asked a question, *"What is the one thing I should do to make things better for you?"* Then he listened.

Dyke followed this with another question, *"What is the one thing I should do to make things better for our viewers and listeners?"*

He knew that at that early stage, he could learn more from his employees than they could from him. The workers at the BBC had many wonderful ideas that they were keen to share. The fact that the new boss took time to question and then listen earned him enormous respect.

All the great inventors and scientists asked questions. Isaac Newton asked, *"Why does an apple fall from a tree?"* and, *"Why does the moon not fall into the Earth?"*

Charles Darwin asked, *"Why do the Galapagos Islands have so many species not found elsewhere?"*

Albert Einstein asked, *"What would the universe look like if I rode through it on a beam of light?"*

By asking these kinds of fundamental questions, these ordinary people were able to start the process that led to their tremendous breakthroughs, which made them extraordinary leaders and legends.

As a mother, I have come to learn that the solutions to most of life's problems lie not in the right answers but the right questions. Children do this right; they are innocently curious and express this through repeated questions. The most famous is the 'WHY' question. The easiest tool for learning is the use of questions. There's an adage where I come from which says that "when you ask for directions, you never miss your way." I am sure you know this to be so true. The key word here is ASK.

Therefore, the leadership alphabet Q is Questioning.

This is an important navigation tool for life. As you know, life is a journey, not a destination, and as a traveller, you need maps to direct you; that is the usefulness of questions. Questioning is a critical skill that successful individuals and great leaders have in common. The courage and ability to make use of the questioning tool will, to a large extent, determine the quality of answers we get in life. You must be willing to ask questions in order to enjoy the journey called 'LIFE.'

Some people are afraid that by asking questions they will look weak, ignorant or unsure. However, asking questions is a sign of strength and intelligence, not a sign of weakness or uncertainty. Great leaders constantly ask questions and are well aware that they do not have all the answers. Just as John C. Maxwell rightly said, *"Good leaders ask great questions."*

From a tender age, we are taught the five 'W' and one 'H' questions: Why, What, Who, When, Where and How. The reason being that our success is dependent on our ability to use these questions.

Some years ago, I experienced a fulfilment gap, and I launched into a quest for my 'Why,' that is, my purpose. Question after question led me into a deep soul searching, and I gradually began to figure out my 'why.' The moment I was clear as to what my purpose is, I then began to figure out the 'how.' Soon after, I figured out the 'when' - time, and of course, the 'who' - those I intend to collaborate with to birth my purpose.

Questions have a way of introducing us to ourselves in terms of our strengths and areas for improvement. When we ask questions, it becomes easy to identify our comfort zone and our capacity zone. Your comfort zone is where you operate at average; your capacity zone is where you perform at the optimal levels. Success is available in the comfort zone, while 'Significance' is achievable only in the capacity zone. A good question to ask is, "Am I doing the best I can?"

Whether as a student, entrepreneur, or employee, you require a questioning environment to thrive. As an employer or manager of people, you are to create this questioning environment. Imagine not being able to ask your teachers questions; how then do you understand? Or not being able to ask your manager and those around you questions! How then do you get clarity to enable you to deliver on goals and tasks successfully? The only way to kill ignorance is to ask questions. Likewise, the only way to deliver great results is to ask questions. Questions are useful daily, in transitions, for projects, and at intersections in life.

Some of the benefits include:
- Questions enrich and add rigour to our thought process.

- It illuminates and enlightens.

- It releases capacity and creativity.

- It enables self-awareness which unlocks potential.

- Questions provide clarity which enables proper allocation of scarce resources.

- It builds relationships.

- Helps challenge the status quo to create a better environment.

- Helps planning.

As you journey through life, always remember it is more important to ask questions than it is to provide answers. The right questions will elicit the right answers.

Exercise:

Ask yourself certain questions daily, such as:

a) What will be the best use of my time today?

b) How will I contribute to my world?

c) What will I do if I knew I would not fail?

d) Who do I need in my circle to be the best I can be?

*Write down your answers to these and other questions you would like to ask yourself.

WORKBOOK

WORKBOOK

It's me...

R:
RESPONSIBILITY

"The price for greatness is Responsibility"
— Winston Churchill.

Some time ago, I had a manager with whom I did not get on well. It seemed I triggered off her worst nature all the time. Not being comfortable with this, I began to observe the team dynamics. I found out that she got on well with every other member of the team except me. The easiest way to explain her behaviour would have been to conclude that she just did not like me or my guts, which is the mindset of a victim. Instead, I decided to look inward, remembering a proverb my grandmother repeatedly told me, *"when you point a finger at someone, the other four fingers point back at you."*

After some self-evaluation, I found out that I was responsible for the way I was treated; I needed to play more as a team member and not be an Island of excellence. Of course, the rest is history; we worked better as a team, and my effort at making a change was appreciated.

How many times have you passed the buck instead of stepping up? Each time we fail to look inward, we miss the opportunity to make an improvement and strengthen character. The process of looking inward is called taking Responsibility.

This bring us to the leadership alphabet R: Responsibility.

Responsibility is being accountable for your thoughts, words and deeds in life. It enables you to keep control of your life. When we live our lives without holding ourselves accountable, then we relinquish control to others. And instead of having and working out our dreams, we wait on the sidelines hoping we can fit into someone else's plan. It is being honest with yourself even when you are wrong. It is the courage to accept your shortcomings, the commitment to improve them and the confidence to push toward your dreams. It is looking inward first, before pointing outward.

In the process of coaching diverse people, I find that the default position of the ordinary mind is to blame someone else for ALL things gone wrong. The hard truth is that except you brace up and take ownership of your life through the lens of responsibility, you may never make the necessary progress in life. Taking responsibility puts you in the driver's seat – you are in control of your time, resources, and plans. In secondary school, I struggled with Mathematics, and I concluded that the problem was the teacher instead of stepping up to learn. I was only fooling myself. If the problem was the teacher, then most of the students should be like me, struggling. But it was the opposite.

You cannot afford to live life as a spectator. Abdicating responsibility is refusing to play the main character in the story of your life. Then you will have to live with the script. Life is not a dress rehearsal; it is the grand performance. Whatever you make of it is what it is. Responsibility is the architect of design; it enables you to create the life you want.

I am sure many of us have read books on transformation, and at the end of the last page, you were not in the least way transformed. Some of us have sat at the feet of great teachers, and speakers and at the end of the event, nothing changed. We were not transformed because we failed to take responsibility. How many times have you said, "I need to achieve a goal," yet you could not bring yourself to initiate the habits that will move you toward your goal?

To make a success of your life, you must take responsibility for your choices. Once you do this, then your choices begin to enable your dreams. Taking or stepping up to responsibility sets you apart from the multitude.

The lyrics of the song, Ire by Adekunle Gold, readily come to mind:

"The grass is greener on the other side, that's what I thought before I took the ride.... the grass is greener when you water the ground, that's what I found when I took the ride."

Responsibility is watering your grass!

Exercise:
a) Are you willing to take responsibility?

b) In what areas of your life do you find it difficult

to take responsibility?

c) Why do you think it is difficult for you to take responsibility?

d) How will you take responsibility?

e) Make a commitment. Write your commitment statement so you never forget.

f) Recite it daily.

****

BONUS WORD

Our bonus word for leadership alphabet R is Respect.

Have you ever concluded that someone does not respect you? What was the evidence? Most likely the way they spoke, looked at you, maybe continuous interruptions, and their general body language. This means that respect is a feeling expressed in actions. It is an essential ingredient in successful relationships. Just like communication, it is a two-way process, and it is reciprocal.

Wikipedia describes Respect as a positive feeling or action shown towards someone or something considered important, or held in high esteem or regard; it conveys a sense of admiration for good or valuable qualities; and it is also the process of honouring someone by exhibiting care, concern, or consideration for their needs or feelings.

Though a derivative of age, position, experience, expertise and socio-economic classifications, respect is beyond these. It is the dignity owed every human being. It is clarity in perspective, which entrenches the fact that everyone has a story and should be listened to. It is the mind shift, which believes that the other person is equally as important or even more important than self. It is the acceptance of the fact that our individuality is an important part of the collective and that every individual carries some value in them. Respect or the absence thereof is easily spotted in our mannerisms.

When we respect self, then it is easy to respect others. After all, you cannot give what you do not have! Respect must be nurtured by the receiver and giver for it to be sustained. Beyond it being the dignity owed every human being, it is also a more profound reciprocal feeling, which is the result of a value-based relationship and interaction with others.

The law of life, which is the golden rule, *"do unto others as you would have them do unto you"* is the law of respect and love. When we love and respect people, we naturally have their ears, and they look out for us. Respect must not be misinterpreted for boot licking. Respect is nurtured by the strength of character. When character fails, then respect is lost.

*What is your perspective on respect?

WORKBOOK

WORKBOOK

S: SERVICE

"Life's most persistent and urgent question is: What are you doing for others?"
— Martin Luther King.

When Garrick, a Southwest Airlines flight attendant, found himself in the position to help a passenger in need, he went above and beyond the call of duty.

Nine-year-old Gabby, a type one diabetic, was severely anxious about being on an airplane. Garrick, a Southwest crew member, worked throughout the flight to make her more comfortable, bringing her special drinks and trying to make her laugh after he noticed her struggling during takeoff.

When the plane hit a serious patch of turbulence, he let her sit in the empty seat next to him, talked to her about his daughter, who is the same age as Gabby, and even let Gabby grab his arm for comfort.

Upon arrival, Garrick used the PA system to tell everyone in the plane that his young friend, Gabby, had just overcome her fear of flying and that she deserved a round of applause from everyone in the plane.

"The whole passengers clapped for her," her mother reported, "it was a wonderful experience, and we are forever grateful to have met such a beautiful, selfless soul."

This singular act got Garrick a well-deserved recognition by Southwest Airlines for his exceptional service, in going above and beyond to help the little girl overcome her fear.

There are few things in life that we enjoy more than seeing one person going out of their way to help another. When a flight attendant goes above and beyond for a frightened passenger, or a cashier helps an elderly man to his car in a rainstorm, you're witnessing something much more than 'good customer service'. Yes, you're actually witnessing exceptional service beyond the expectations of his or her job description to make a customer's day, and that's an integral part of life that should never be forgotten to lead successfully.

This brings us to the leadership alphabet S, which is Service.

Two decades of my career have been in the service industry. Though in different sectors, my core has remained Customer Experience. Service is about the customer. It is about coming up with value-adding propositions for the customer. Organizations understand that their relevance is assured to the extent that they can meet the customers' needs in one way or the other. Service is adding value to someone else. And yes, it is never about you but someone else. Service as a virtue is unique; it is only in service that giving does not deplete you, but it increases you. Thus, it is one of the significant keys to succeeding with your venture and overall success in life. As Shep Hyken affirms, *"All of your customers are partners in your mission"* in life.

Our lives will only be remembered in the context of our service to others; our legacies only described in the way we impacted others. Have you ever attended a commendation service? You will notice that the speakers' perspective is often based on personal encounters with the commended. Service is giving back to others and society. It is lending yourself to your community (family, team, society, etc.) by proffering solutions which solve or minimize the problems that abound in our society and the world at large. Service is a mix of the soft and hard stuff – from helping a child or the aged cross the road, mentoring, coaching, sponsoring a child through school to innovations that move the quality and standard of life to the next level. Service is not conspiring with silence to destroy the society; it is speaking up against the vices that stealthily and steadily destroy the environment in which we should thrive.

Tim Fargo couldn't be more direct when he said, *"Leadership is service, not position."* I am reminded of great men and women: Mother Theresa, Martin Luther King Jnr, Harriet Tubman, Rosa Parks, Helen Keller, Nelson Mandela, Mahatma Gandhi, to mention a few. These lived a life of service; the problems of the society in which they lived, be it health, slavery, apartheid, became the cause they lived for and in some cases eventually died for; likewise, organizations such as the Bill and Melinda Foundation. Today, we continue to remember these men and women who moved society closer to realising its potentials because of their service.

Service is vital in leadership; thus, if serving is below

you, then leadership is beyond you. The simplest way to lead by example is to serve others. Does your community feel your impact, or are you so consumed by the daily pressures of life that you feel you should live for yourself? You see, our environment will only yield back to us what we put into it. As a young girl, I spent much time with my grandmother, whom we all called *'Moomi'*, meaning 'my mother.' She taught me that when your neighbour is fine, then you are fine, and Vice-Versa.

I work for a multinational organisation that encourages all their employees across the different countries to give back to the host communities using our time, affiliations, money and intellect. For the past 15 years, the first 21 days of June every year is dedicated to service. It has helped us imbibe a culture of Individual Social Responsibility (ISR). For some of us, it continues to be a life-transforming opportunity.

Service is a great way to build true relationships and to make a difference. The more you serve or help others, the more your circle of influence widens, and the value of your social capital deepens. In an HBR article, *"Service-Based Leadership,"* Angie Morgan and Courtney Lynch discuss this form of leadership unique to the U.S. Marines. The Marine superior officers prioritized their team's needs before their own. As superiors they always ate last, ensuring first that their team members had food on their plates and well-fed before theirs were filled. When it was dark and cold in the field, the superiors made a point of being out there with their teams and serving their needs, not laying cozy in a warm tent. The duo found that superiors leading by service made team members feel valued, and this was reciprocated through team member loyalty and engagement.

The highest type of service is selfless service. Spend your energy serving others. If you do not do this, then you might struggle with a future you did not prevent. Service empowers you to create an environment that enables you. It is the DNA of great leaders; leadership is all about service.

Exercise:
a) Are you currently serving in any capacity in your family, school, and community?

b) If no, why not?

c) If yes, what are some of the things you have

done to impact your community?

d) In what capacity would you like to serve?

e) Start serving through volunteer programs.

WORKBOOK

T:
TIME

"Don't be fooled by the calendar. There are only as many days in the year as you make use of. One man gets only a week's value out of a year while another man gets a full year's value"
— Anthony Charles Richards.

Nancy was habitually late with submitting her course work assignments, no matter the amount of time she had to get it done, and consequently had to lose some points on the course, which negatively impacts her overall grades. She always attributed her lateness to "having no time."

Frustrated with her outcomes, she asked her Professor, *"How can I manage my time? I feel like 24* hours is no longer enough for me, with so much to do."

Professor Lynn started by saying that there is a thumb rule of this world for time management; focused people have no problem with time because they make time work for them, but that people who lack a sense of priority will always have less or no time because they often spend their days killing time with unimportant tasks, thus achieve little or nothing in the end. So, in reality, everyone has enough time since everyone has the same 24 hours. People only do not know how to use it.

"Ever heard of Benjamin Franklin?" Professor Lynn asked.

"Yes; but not as it relates to this issue," Nancy replied, confused.

"Ok. As a young man in his twenties, Benjamin Franklin was a very hardworking man, but no matter how hard he worked each day, the employers still complained that he was not getting much done, and thus, was not productive. So, Franklin started observing himself. He got a diary and made a list, categorizing his daily tasks into 'important', 'less important', 'least important', and 'avoidable tasks'. At the end of each day, Franklin would check off tasks that he had completed."

"After a week, he observed that he worked on 'less important' and 'avoidable tasks' more than the important tasks. He discovered firsthand how he was wasting valuable time, achieving things that did not matter. Little wonder his employers complained he was not productive, despite how hardworking he was. With this new insight, Franklin began to think more about what it means to be productive and how to achieve it, seeing it was quite different from being hardworking. This led him to learn and practice how to prioritize, thereby, manage his time more effectively."

Professor Lynn summarized, saying that Benjamin Franklin eventually became the man who got much done. He was a leading Author, Printer, Political Theorist, Politician, Postmaster, Scientist, Musician, Inventor, Satirist, Civic Activist, Statesman, and Diplomat; in addition to being one of the United States of America's founding fathers, who helped draft the Declaration of Independence and the U.S. Constitution.

For many, the lines blur between being productive and being hardworking because many do not prioritize and are not aware that some tasks can be avoided or left for later. Hence, at the end of the day, they don't feel like they have achieved much, yet they feel exhausted. If we make a habit of 'no compromise' with "important tasks", it becomes easier to optimise our time.

Thus, the leadership Alphabet T is TIME!

Life will always be a function of time – past, present and future, expressed in time – Age, and lived in time – minute, hour, day, week, and year. Time is the currency of life. What you get or do not get out of life is directly related to how you make use of your time.

I particularly love the way Wikipedia defines time: *"Time is the indefinite continued progress of existence and events that occur in apparently irreversible succession from the past through the present to the future."* The word irreversible in the definition surely resonates with me. It means that time is on a mission and continues on this mission regardless of what we do or do not do with it. I remember a popular Nigerian musician in the '90s, Mike Okri. He titled one of his songs *'Time Na Moni'* (as spoken in pidgin English) which means 'Time is Money.' In the song, he advises that time be used for valuable activities. Just as Mohammed Bin Rashid Al Maktoum rightly puts it, *"Time is like a flowing river: you cannot step into the same water twice."*

Our priorities, energy and self can be controlled but not time. Time is a resource that must be spent in the achievement of identified goals; the outcome of the use of your time is dependent on knowing what goals you are working to achieve because precise time schedule helps make your goals achievable. It is an enabler. The best use of time is to use it in order of priority! The more you use time in a focused and intentional manner, the more you can create time for other things and start ahead; this is what we often describe as being Proactive. You will never have time if you don't create the needed time in order of priority!

Here are some truths about time:
• Time can only be spent and not saved; spend your time doing meaningful things.

• The more you spend time wisely, the more it compounds.

• Purpose + self-mastery + Time = success.

• When time is put to good use, productivity is high, and the probability of burnout and stress is reduced.

What do you spend your time on? I have met people whose achievements equate them with aliens, suggesting that they are blessed with more than 24 hours in a day. John C. Maxwell, in his book

'No Limits,' recommends building our discipline capacity in order to get more out of our 24 hours. Self-discipline is the ability to commit to your plans. Paul Martinelli describes it as *"the ability to give yourself a command and obey it"*. Self-discipline is a daily craft.

Success is never measured by the number of hours available to you in a day but by the quality of your results and outcomes. Regardless of the season of life that we are in – youth, middle age, old age, what we do and continue to do with time will define how seamless the transition to the next season will be; it will determine how fulfilled and productive we become. Your productivity is always directly proportional to how you appropriate time.

I often hear people moan and complain "there isn't enough time in a day", "my schedule is too crowded", "I am always firefighting", "it is difficult for me to achieve work-life balance", and so on. How does one achieve work-life balance when 80 percent of our time is spent on activities that give us only 20 percent value? The 80/20 Pareto rule holds sway when it comes to time. It is established that only 20 percent of what we do births 80 percent of our impact. So, why don't we spend our time on the big-ticket items? Use your time to create more balance in your life. It is this balance that puts you in the driver's seat of your life.

Below are some nuggets that may help you in achieving more with your time:
- Have a vision: write it down and memorize it.

- Distill the vision into SMART goals:
    S – Specific
    M – Measurable
    A – Achievable
    R – Realistic
    T – Time-bound.

- From your goals, identify your Big-ticket actions; these should be the actions that leapfrog you and make a difference.

- Prioritize your Big-tickets by committing your time to the achievement.

- Plan your day, week, month and year ahead. Be intentional with your time.

- Consciously change a daily habit.

- Get an accountability partner; someone who wishes you well and can hold you to your commitment.

One good thing is that it is never too late to spend your time well. You can start TODAY!!!

Exercise:

a) How would you appropriate time in establishing your purpose?

b) Draw a table categorizing your daily tasks into 'important', 'less important', 'least important', and 'avoidable tasks. Each day check off what you got done from the list.

c) Identify and write down your daily energy drainers. Work on eliminating them as much as you can.

U:
URGENCY

"Without a sense of urgency, desire loses its value"
— Jim Ron.

In high school, Kelly's basketball Coach would often say, "speed is the name of the game." Her Coach brought it up repeatedly and made the team members chant it before every practice and game. Kelly was a little below average height in high school, and so wasn't a girl anyone would have easily considered for basketball, but she turned out to be one of the best in the school district, because where she came short in height, she made up for speed and agility, which earned her the position of team captain.

Subsequently, she began to apply those words to every aspect of life as she discovered the more profound meaning and power of the words. What she learned about it from hearing and chanting it for so many years is that it holds the same amount of truth in life, business and leadership, as it does in basketball — the urgency in pursuit of a goal matters. Doing quality work will always be a top priority, but urgency delivers the goal right on time.

Early on, Kelly understood that people who live with a sense of urgency, also live their lives with purpose and meaning, so procrastination or a sluggish attitude was something she decided was never an option for her. Thus, she wakes up each day with a purpose for the day, possessing an inner urgency that drives her to deliver on it, even on the basketball court.

Several years after, Kelly witnessed most of her basketball team members in high school, allow procrastination and a sluggish attitude in their personal or professional lives sabotage their success and stump their growth, as they forgot or never considered that the secret weapon, which is often overlooked, to one's personal and professional success is that sense of urgency. That sense of urgency became the great asset that propelled Kelly to the peak of her career, above her peers.

Consequently, Kelly wondered why urgency is rarely talked about when discussing all of the required characteristics that make up the highly successful. Yet, without a doubt, it is a critical requirement in the pursuit of achieving one's goals because the rate of change in today's world is going up at lightning speed. However, just like her team members, everyone says it, but very few people believe it.

Therefore, the leadership alphabet U is Urgency!

Have you ever had an idea or a strong urge to do something? At times it's something big, it's never been done before. At other times it's ordinary. What did you do with the idea? Severally, I have had ideas – the Universal Mind releases ideas in bursts from time to time. I observed that the conception of an idea is usually accompanied by an overwhelming urge to birth the idea. I have also observed that the longer you hold onto the idea, the faster the urge wanes. From my personal experience, the moment I do nothing about the idea, I lose the urge to run with it and then gradually, I let go. But guess what? In a few weeks or months, I see the same idea as a finished product, owned by someone else. Someone who defied the odds and ran with it, someone who understood the importance of seizing the moment, someone with a sense of urgency. Whenever this happens, I remember my dad, who always said to me, *"no one thinks in isolation. Whenever you think, make sure you DO."*

Once the urge wanes without birthing the idea, you lose both the will and the energy to go on. You beat yourself up for being lazy. In my life as a corporate citizen, I have sent a litany of emails to my colleagues ending with "Please treat as very urgent", hoping this would enable the recipient to take action. In some instances, it spurs my colleagues to action; in other instances, they could not be bothered. A sense of urgency makes all the difference between a dreamer and an achiever.

Many of us are unfulfilled, dissatisfied and feel unaccomplished because we fail to respond to ideas and opportunities which repeatedly come our way. In other words, we fail to approach our visions, goals and dreams with the required sense of urgency, so we end up frustrated and envious of other people's accomplishments. A sense of urgency makes all the difference between a dreamer and an achiever. In the words of the famous Chinese proverb, *"the best time to plant a tree was 20 years ago, the second-best time is now."* Life must be lived with a sense of urgency, knowing fully well that today will never come again; there will be other days, but today will never be again.

Our dreams elude us because we fail to take action, and we fail to take action because of the following:

- **Fear:** We worry about what others will say, the truth is that they are not watching. We ponder on the possibility of failure and remain in a state of inertia. We think the idea is common and we might be tagged 'copycat.' Ask yourself this question again, "if you are Thomas Edison would you have invented the light bulb?" Dear friend, you need to douse the intensity of fear by creating a sense of urgency and reaffirming to yourself the fact that you have been equipped with all that you need.

Self-limiting beliefs: *"I am not good enough", "I don't have the right qualifications", "my background works against me"*, are some of the limiting beliefs some have embraced over time. You have believed these lies for too long. Refuse to be a function of other people's dysfunction. Practice self-accelerating confessions; tell yourself the positive opposites of these things and beyond that, believe them. You need to validate yourself.

- **Analysis paralysis:** Because we prioritize the fear of failure, we are afraid to take the leap; time is wasted trying to analyze the risks and play safe. Then we become rooted in the same spot until we lose the will to execute. Stop over analyzing, start doing, *"with action comes clarity."* – Melissa West.

- **Procrastination:** This is the delusion that we are in charge, and so tomorrow is guaranteed. Therefore, we become lazy with today believing that we'll catch up tomorrow. When we procrastinate, our urgency gives way to later. We become overwhelmed with piles of 'to do', and of course, nothing gets done. John C. Maxwell, in his book, *'the 15 Laws of Growth'* describes it as the law of diminishing intent which simply means "the more you hang on to something the higher the chances of not doing it." Live today like it's your last. Birth your ideas with passion; that idea may change the world!

Here are some ways to nurture your sense of urgency:

- **Acknowledge the idea:** Let it play in your mind. Think about it. Visualize it. Steven Covey says, *"Begin with the end in mind."*

- **Write it down:** The first step in actualizing a dream is putting it down in words. Write the goal; keep it where you can see it. This helps you own it.

- **Break it down into tiny bits:** This is necessary to avoid feeling overwhelmed. It will help you manage your energy.

- **Share your dream with like-minded people:** When you say it, it becomes difficult to renege. These people can become your accountability partners, and they enable your journey.

- **Collaborate:** You are one person and cannot do everything. Look for people who will enable the dream, e.g. graphic artists, website builders, volunteers, writers, individuals with complementary skills. This makes it easy to jump-start the dream. I leave you with this as food for thought: "When you become, you encourage others to be."

Exercise:

What will you do starting from NOW? Write them down as a constant reminder.

WORKBOOK

WORKBOOK

V: VALUE

"What you do makes a difference, and you have to decide what kind of difference you want to make"
— Jane Goodall.

The Dim company executives sit in the boardroom to decide necessary layoff in the customer support department; they need to layoff one person out of the six, and so gradually narrow the options down to two employees:

Option A: "Edward" is an old and faithful company standby. He's worked at the company for 15 years and has been completely faithful to his job expectations. He gets in and out on time and delivers his customer support perfectly on the script. As a result, he's accumulated a number of raises over the years and now makes $25 an hour.

Option B: "Tony" has only worked in customer support for five years but has obtained advanced technical certifications, has an excellent interpersonal manner, and routinely turns upset customers into loyal patrons. Clients who get support from him are 35 percent more likely to purchase additional services and to refer friends. He talks off the script a fair amount of time but keeps track of what he says and how customers react. As a result, he has submitted many helpful modifications to the basic customer support script, resulting in a 15 percent increase in customer satisfaction for the whole department. Due to his high performance, Tony also makes $25 per hour, same as Edward.

"Which one gets fired?" The Managing Director asked.

"It's Edward without question," answered the Human Resource Director.

"Why?"

"Edward's problem is that he hasn't really done anything to justify his increased wages; he has made

no significant improvement to either the company or himself in his 15 years here. Small raises have accumulated on his paycheck over the years like dust on an unused desk, but his real value is still around $12.50 per hour as when he was first hired. The company is actually losing money on Edward. If we fire him, a new employee would work for only $12.50 per hour and could read the script, just as skillfully as Edward, within two weeks."

"However, if Tony is fired, the company would lose out on a major source of sales, referrals, customer satisfaction and an internal system for improving the whole department; we can't afford to lose him."

So, the leadership alphabet V is Value.

I make it a point to remind myself and those around me that the game of life is that of relevance. I am also quick to follow up with the statement, *"you are as relevant as the value you bring to the table."* Value borders on the advantages and benefits that you are able to create for people in the course of your interaction with them and vice versa. The essence of life is to make better, to create and re-make. Value is very important. OUR SINGULAR PURPOSE IN LIFE IS TO ADD VALUE to people, situations, contexts, etc. It is to be M.A.D. (Making A Difference). Did you know that human beings are ever only described in terms of the value they have added to others! Value is a two-sided coin; you must give it to get it.

The search for purpose sees every human being evolve through three stages in life: survival, success, and significance. At the survival stage, life is pretty much happening to you; life is living you instead of you living life. You are struggling to find your purpose and passion in life. You are directed and pretty much controlled by the need to survive in the immediate. The mindset in this stage is, at best, short and myopic. At this level, it takes a lot of awareness and self-discipline to navigate the bend that leads to success. A basic to intermediate proficiency in self-mastery will enable the exit into the 'success' stage.

The success stage is characterized by a consuming obsession with oneself. At this point, one's focus is to establish purpose. Here, we talk of vision statements, goal setting and skill development. At this stage, humans desire achievement and attainment for self; it could be a degree, incremental knowledge, dexterity of skills, etc. The thought process and the mindset begin to shift into the mid-term to long-term mode. Goals are set in the long-term frame. The driving force at the success level is largely self. Expert proficiency in self-mastery and awareness opens the door of significance.

Significance is about adding value to others than oneself. It is beyond self. Characterized by the need to take on a bigger adversary to enable the purpose of others. At this stage, the desire for self fades away while the obsession with making positive change in every context sets in. Significance is all about adding value to people. Remember value is a two-sided coin, you must give it to get it. The mindset here is very long term, even after one is gone. It is about solving problems for the benefit of others.

The capacity to create value for and add value to others is where our fulfilment lies. Corporate Organizations remain relevant and profitable to the extent that they can add value to and create value for their customers. The more they can predict the customer behaviour, the more they can create value for the customers and the longer they remain in business. Some of the greatest humans of our time have attained significance - Steve Jobs was great because he chose to add value to people through technology, entertainment, and research. Jeff Bezos transformed the retail space by using technology and connectedness to influence Customer Behaviour. Bill Gates is living beyond himself, raising the health standards of various African countries and contributing to various researches.

Adding value to others launches an inquest into the capabilities and capacity of the human mind resulting in the birthing of significant innovations. At the stage of significance, Richard Branson couldn't be more accurate when he said, *"Don't think about making money, think about making a difference, spot where others are doing it badly and do it better."*

Upon each life is the calling to make a difference, to add and create value. To live a truly fulfilled life, we must transit from survival to success and then to significance. We must add value to others, be the solutions to the questions of others. As Seth Godin puts it, *"not adding value is the same thing as taking it away."* As you make it a habit to add value to others, please look back and say thank you to those that have added value to you.

Exercise:
a) What is your understanding of value?

b) In your opinion, do you think Edward should be fired? If no, why?

c) Write about something someone did for you that

you consider as adding value to you.

d) How will you add value to others today?

e) Who will you make a difference in their life today?

WORKBOOK

WORKBOOK

W: WIN-WIN

"The true test of character is to live win-win even when promoted to positions where win-lose is possible"
— Orrin Woodward.

A few years back, Iminathi was driving to a meeting in Pretoria to bid for a multi-million dollar contract, there was much traffic, and then no parking space left, which got her more agitated than she already was, having been told severally she had zero chance of getting the contract. So, rather than drive around in the traffic looking for parking space, she drove across to a nearby five-star hotel with Valet parking.

What happened next was so unexpected; Iminathi

opened her door to hand over her car keys to the Valet, and she was blown away by his enthusiasm, much that she thought he had just won a $100 million lottery; his energy was off the charts. He was a total powerhouse of pure joy. He greeted her as if he was picking up some lifelong friend at the airport, then he gently helped her out of her car and asked her about her day. And guess what? He was genuinely interested in her answer, and then he flashed this smile at her that was brighter than the hot afternoon sunlight. This man was one of the most enthusiastic souls Iminathi had ever met.

Now, what struck Iminathi was that this was the Valet, not the Managing Director, and as someone who has worked in the service industry for years, she knew that this kind of job could be very challenging; often dealing with all kinds of cranky people; probably not making that much money, and sometimes, it can be thankless, but clearly none of that bothered this man. The energy he brought to his work was more like he was this happy king who was welcoming people into his palace.

That afternoon, with her confidence and self-esteem boosted, Iminathi walked into that meeting with a confident smile, feeling like she already won the contract, despite the odds against her, and three hours later, she walked out of that meeting with a winning smile, having won the contract. Her encounter with this man with a winning mentality that translated into his infectious positive energy paid off.

Iminathi considered the fact that the Valet could have used his position and the challenges of his work as an excuse to ruin every customer's day, but he chose to be positively influential, clearly proving the point that when you win, he wins because no one will so easily forget such a personality and his impact on her outcome.

That day, Iminathi realized how contagious energy is, and since then, carefully considers what she wants people to catch from her, especially as a leader. She learnt a valuable lesson always to be win-win conscious. When your actions have a direct influence on the outcomes for you and others around you, it is vital always to strive to create winning situations, not a win-lose or lose-lose.

Thus, the leadership alphabet W is Win-Win.

The above story is the simplest illustration of a win-win situation. Iminathi's experience with the Valet is the most potent reminder of one of the most underrated secrets for how to be successful in life. The energy, the soul, the spirit that you infuse into your actions matter; to win in life, you must feel and act like you are a winner, much that others can catch the fire from you and know they can win too.

Win-Win is a mindset, a situation where the outcome elevates the state of being of those involved – individual, family, society, community. A win-win mindset is making sure that our outcomes are a result of awareness of others and the environment. We are raised to believe that our victory is dependent on someone else's loss; our success is the outcome of someone else's failure. The general belief is that there is not enough for all and so we must 'by all means and at all costs' get what we can, even though it might mean hurting others and being unkind. In other words, we are nurtured to have a scarcity mindset.

In his book, *'Seven Habits of Highly Effective People,'* Stephen Covey describes the fourth habit, 'Think Win-Win' as *"a frame of mind and heart that constantly seeks mutual benefit in ALL human interrelations."*

The win-win mindset is an abundance mindset. This mindset believes that there is more than enough or at least enough for all. It holds true to the fact that for me to succeed does not mean you have to fail. It believes 'we' can all achieve, that 'we' have all been fully endowed with all we need. The abundance mindset sees possibilities, while the scarcity mindset sees impossibilities. This manifests in the attitudes and perspectives of these two extremes on the spectrum of life.

Abundance originates from faith and scarcity, from fear. Remember, the law of life is, *"the more you give, the more you receive."* This is because nature is programmed to respond to the win-win mindset over the scarcity mindset. Abundance thinking is 'an out of the comfort zone' positioning. Our breakthroughs, dreams, and purpose are usually found outside our comfort zone. An abundance mindset understands that to grow is to pour out oneself for a cause. The win-win mindset is a generous one.

Belief drives behaviour and behaviour fuels outcomes. Great humans such as the Wright brothers, Thomas Edison, Steve Jobs, Bill Gates, all operated from the abundance perspective. Everything they did was to raise the standard and quality of life. I recall when I was in school, there was a general belief that you do not share knowledge because the more you share, the more your knowledge diminishes. Truth is I discovered it was the other way around. I discovered that sharing knowledge helps me win because I understand and retain more. So, I would often organize tutorials for my classmates – we won together. I got better, and they also increased in knowledge.

Another example is from the Bible, about the little boy with five loaves and two fishes: he could have kept his lunch to himself while everyone goes hungry, but instead, he gave it to Jesus, it was multiplied, and everyone benefited. A win-win mindset strengthens your character and increases your authenticity and credibility. People trust you because you genuinely lookout for them.

It is important for you to know that a win-win does not translate to giving up your dreams and plans because of others. What it means is that your decisions and actions, dreams and plans must positively elevate the whole community of which you are a part.

Exercise:
a) Visualize a home with 12 children, and they have to share a box of Pizza amongst themselves. Now, remember they are all hungry. Which of the following options (1 - 4) do you think would apply and reflect a win-win mindset?

1. **Winner takes it all:** this probably means only about three or four of them will have the pizza. If you choose this option, explain why you chose it.

2. **Share according to age:** the pizza will reach more children, with the older ones getting bigger portions. If you choose this option, explain why you chose it.

3. **Decide not to eat the pizza:** If you choose this option, explain why you chose it.

4. **Decide to share the pizza with everyone having an equal portion:** If you choose this option, explain why you chose it.

b) How will you use the win-win as a daily tool?

c) Describe a situation when you used or plan to use the win-win mindset.

d) Share a win-win situation with others around you and encourage them to apply it in their lives.

WORKBOOK

WORKBOOK

X:
X FACTOR

"Go the extra mile because doing your best in this moment puts you in the best place for the next moment"
— Oprah Winfrey.

Apple is one of the most successful companies in the world, which changed the way we live and use technology today. Apple's most notable leader was the late CEO, Steve Jobs. In an article written by Carmine Gallo, *"The Seven Success Principles of Steve Jobs,"* he outlined seven key factors that were responsible for Jobs' success. The article was based on interviews with Apple employees and Steve Jobs himself. The first principle Gallo listed in the article is, *"Do what you love."* Steve Jobs believed in the power of passion and thus, once said, *"People with passion can change the world for the better."* Jobs claimed that the passion he had for his work made all the difference.

Mark Zuckerberg, Facebook's CEO, changed the world in which we live. In David Kirkpatrick's book, *"The Facebook Effect: The Inside Story of the Company That is Connecting the World,"* Kirkpatrick lists the qualities that led to Zuckerberg's success. Top of the list is following his passion, not money. Moreover, Zuckerberg, in his own words said, *"following your happiness,"* using the logic that even if you do not end up making a fortune, you will at least be doing what you love and touching the world.

Chris Gardner, the once-homeless man, turned multi-millionaire stockbroker, and featured in the movie, *"The Pursuit of Happiness,"* expressed what he believes is the secret to success. According to Gardner, the secret is to *"find something you love to do so much you can't wait for the sun to rise to do it all over again."* He explains that the most inspiring leaders are those who do not work but pursue a calling, and in it make the world a better place for all.

The distinctive factor that sets organisations and

individuals apart is unique for each organisation and person. But in nearly all cases, it has to do with passion and the approach as it relates to people. Pay attention to the unique common trait with each of these great leaders. They all had something in common: they absolutely *'love and have passion'* for what they do, and they *'solve problems'* thereby, *'creating solutions'* that *'elevate the standards of human'* existence - they are people-centred; money or personal gain was never the deciding factor for them. The 'passion' to 'make the world work better for all' and to 'improve the lives of people' drove them. As Alan Armstrong puts it, *"If there is no passion in your life, then have you really lived? Find your passion, whatever it may be. Become it, and let it become you and you will find great things happen FOR you, TO you and BECAUSE of YOU."* That made these great leaders indispensable and a force to reckon with.

This brings us to the leadership alphabet X, which is X Factor.

X Factor is defined as a noteworthy special talent, quality, or circumstance that has a strong but unpredictable influence *(Merriam-Webster dictionary)*. The passion with which 'you use' that unique talent or quality, not money-driven, but excellence and people-driven to make the world better - that is the X factor. That X factor changes the world and forces wealth to chase after you, not the other way around; it may appear ordinary to you at first, but it's no ordinary thing: That is the X factor's 'unpredictable influence.'

Talent or a unique quality is nothing without the passion for fueling it, and after it is fueled if it lacks that quality to solve problems or meet needs and impact the world positively, it slowly dies a natural death; there exists no X factor without a positive impact on the world. The X factor will always meet the first law to man about the universe: *"replenish the world"*; it must always add to or benefit the world, not take away from it or leave it worse off.

I am sure you know about the popular talent show 'the X factor.' Over the years the show has become synonymous with displaying talents, uniqueness, specialties and gifts. You get air time on the show when you can convince the judges that you have the X factor, but the moment you sound unappealing, you are cut short because an X factor creates a certain kind of appeal and positive impact on the intended audience, however strange it may appear in some cases. Many of us have the 'X factor'; we just need to discover what it is. We all possess talents and gifts that are locked down within us and waiting to emerge if and when we permit them to be expressed in our lives.

On a more personal level, the X factor also represents that extra that we put into our work, words, and thoughts which enables us to be above and beyond the average. The extra represents discipline, commitment, thoroughness, excellence, and compassion that goes into all that represents us. The world is full of average and mediocre people, which is the direct result of not wanting to go outside our comfort zones, not wanting to stretch ourselves, not wanting to endure the pain of growth to reap the bloom of maturity. Every aspiration, ambition, or dream you will ever have requires work before it can become a reality. The work means we focus our energy on getting things done excellently first, rather than on making money first, but that is what many of us run away from. Just like I hear many often say, *"Is it excellence that will feed me? Just make the work look fair enough, nobody will notice, I'm here to make money."* With this attitude, we bury that X factor that attracts the wealth.

There are many differences between successful people and unsuccessful people; one more is the X factor. Successful people recognize that they cannot go far without bringing on their A-game. They sweat the X factor. They rise above average and commit themselves to excellence in all they do. I am sure you know that average students don't get scholarships. Scholarships are given to those who bring on the X factor. Winners win because they live on the extra mile, they worked their craft and delivered in a way that only geniuses do. Making the extra a way of life gives you an edge over others. You deliver quality and beauty in all you do.

The X factor is a tool for competitive advantage. Many organizations raise the bar delivering high quality products, not once, but at all times. This endears them to their customers, and they remain in business for much longer after their competitors have closed shop. Same applies to individuals; the more you make the 'extra' a way of life, the better you get at delivering world-class outcomes. As the popular saying goes, *"it is less crowded along the extra mile."* These are some well-known individuals who had the X factor: Bill Gates, Steve Jobs, Oprah Winfrey, Mike Zuckerberg, Nelson Mandela, Mahatma Gandhi, Martin Luther king, Jr., Mozart, Leonardo Da Vinci, the Wright brothers, Albert Einstein, Aristotle, Isaac Newton, etc. These replenished, improved, and changed the world with their unique extra touch.

Let these ordinary but great people be the living, potent evidence that your X factor is possible and that you can make things happen. Practicing the extra mile discipline enables your creativity, helps you identify the opportunities and makes you embrace challenges because you are most comfortable outside your comfort zone. Do more, love more, smile more, learn more, apply yourself more. Like a fellow coach, would say, *"Wake up, dress up, and show up."*

Exercise:

a) What is your X-Factor? How do you or can you stand out from everyone else?

c) Make a list of the things you enjoy doing.

d) If many, narrow the list down to three that you think are most important to you.

e) Narrow down the three to one that you will like to achieve first?

f) Write down what extra efforts you will make to become the best at this.

g) Start reading books and materials that teach you about your passion or area of interest.

WORKBOOK

WORKBOOK

WORKBOOK

WORKBOOK

Y: YOU

"To be yourself in a world that is constantly trying to make You something else is the greatest accomplishment"
– Ralph Waldo Emerson.

Jesse, 32 years old, is a director at a global technology company and a part of the prestigious Emerging Leader program. As a child, all Jesse wanted to be was a teacher. He even went as far as getting his parents to put a Blackboard in his room so that he could play "pretend teacher".

Jesse grew up influenced by his parents' dreams for him, family, friends, peer pressure, the media and movies; all of that changed his focus from teaching to landing a "cool job" that comes with much money, title, and prestige. He went on to do his master's degree in Computer Science and became a computer programmer. He was doing what he thought he was supposed to do and what he went to school to study.

"In this role, I was not happy; I felt empty and unfulfilled, and everyone could tell," Jesse said. *"This led me to a self-discovery process that was not easy. I really needed to find myself; to critically look at who I am, what I wanted, what I am good and not good at, and what really makes me happy,"* Jesse continued.

Consequently, Jesse got a new job as a Technical Trainer, teaching people better ways of solving business problems through technology. This was when the light bulb lit up for him, illuminating his darkness, and he embraced himself in all of his uniqueness, leading him full circle back to his personal purpose: teaching and developing people. Jesse finally found the happiness and fulfilment he had been seeking, along with all the other added benefits.

This brings us to the leadership alphabet Y: You.

Yes, YOU! You are special and unique. And as Oscar Wilde directly puts it, *"Be You [yourself]; everyone else is already taken."* You are a fantastic masterpiece with the capacity and ability to do great things. You have great dreams and plans to change the world. The uniqueness of the human mind is unrivalled. I always like to say that the human mind is the greatest magnet ever created. Our minds are limitless, full of greatness and creativity. You are more than you think. The greatness referred to here is available in each one of us in equal measure. It is regardless of where we are from, or where we have been.

Let's try this: If your life was a movie, what genre would it be – thriller, tragedy, adventure, love, drama, or sci-fi? Indeed, our lives are movies, and guess what? We are the lead character in the movie of our lives. You are a superstar! The bonus is that, unlike the Hollywood scripts where the actor most times has no influence on the story, you are fully in charge of your story. You are the scriptwriter, producer and director. From time to time, you recruit additional cast in the form of friends, colleagues, mentors, coaches. In a nutshell, YOU determine the outcome.

Being the lead character comes with responsibilities. Only you can determine the outcome of your story. You are the only one who can give your dreams the permission to become. Don't leave your story to chance. No script is handed over at birth; at best we all got a blank canvas to illustrate the story of our lives. We also got a journal to write our stories. Our actions and inactions combine together to form our story. How is your story unfolding?

Some of the lead character responsibilities include:

- **Have a clear sense of self-awareness:** Positive self-image; know your strengths and work on the areas for improvement. Have a vision born out of a trusted conviction.

- **Have the right mindset:** Read the topic on alphabet M - Mindtitude again, to be reminded of the need to have a positive mindset.

- **Nurture great health habits:** Maintain a proper diet, have a good exercise regimen, good personal hygiene habits, practice gratitude, surround yourself with positive people who can loan you their faith when yours is weak.

- **Use the power of your emotions positively:** Consciously give up negative emotions such as anger, bitterness. Embrace positive emotions of love, joy, forgiveness.

- **Build up your spirituality:** Connect more with your inner self through deliberate affirmations and imaginative thinking, create serenity around you, journaling, and connect with God through prayer.

As you progress in your journey of life, you will encounter obstacles of different forms. These obstacles are not meant to tear you down; they are meant to re-introduce you to your great inner self. They help shape your stories and sharpen your focus. Your trusted conviction and confidence will carry you through the good and not so good times. Marianne Williamson couldn't have said it any better, *"Our deepest fear is not that we are inadequate. Our deepest fear is that we are powerful beyond measure. It is our light, not our darkness that most frightens us. We ask ourselves, 'Who am I to be brilliant, gorgeous, talented, fabulous?' Actually, who are you not to be? You are a child of God. Your playing small does not serve the world. There is nothing enlightened about shrinking so that other people won't feel insecure around you. We are all meant to shine, as children do. We were born to make manifest the glory of God that is within us. It's not just in some of us; it's in everyone. And as we let our own light shine, we unconsciously give other people permission to do the same. As we are liberated from our own fear, our presence automatically liberates others."*

Indeed, you and I are powerful beyond measure. This is expressed in our ability to give life to our dreams and our ability to create iterative solutions that elevate the human existence. For every time you believe you are not enough, for every time you give up on yourself, for every time you fear your greatness, you make the world a poorer place; you diminish humanity's capacity to birth great things. Never let the seeds of self-doubt take root in you. Practice contra accelerating beliefs, i.e. for every self-limiting belief or thought, you introduce the exact opposite of that thought in positivity. Remember that great minds like Thomas Edison, Alexander Graham Bell, Leonardo da Vinci, Mother Theresa, Henry Ford, Walt Disney, and many more starved their fears and fed their faith in their dreams and abilities. They imbibed the discipline of bringing forth, knowing fully well that they are the only ones that can birth or abort their dreams. They cultivated rare levels of accountability.

You see, when I was much younger, I did not like my name even though it has a beautiful meaning, *'the year of joy'*. It was very uncommon. I wanted a more common name. I refused to accept my uniqueness and wanted to be like every other person. As I matured and came in frequent contact with my inner self, I asked my dad why he christened me Odunayo; he told me one of the greatest stories I ever heard. He told me how my birth was the best gift they had received in that tough year. He told me of how I brought a ray of hope into their lives. That day my self-belief received strength, and I have never looked back. I no longer want to be like another because the others are already taken; only me can be me!

All I am saying is that YOU have been resourced with all that you need to express greatness. Never doubt your ability to do big things. You are a force for good, so activate yourself. Remember, take good care of yourself, the world needs you!

Exercise:
a) Take a mirror, look into it and describe what or whom you see? Write this description down.

b) Do you love yourself? Whatever your answer is, why?

c) What do you need to increase your self-love?

d) Work on a positive affirmation you will recite daily for the next 40 days.

WORKBOOK

Z: ZEST

"To truly have a zest for life, you must squeeze all the juice out of it, especially the lemons. Believe it or not, they make life even more delicious. The lessons you get out of them make you strong, resilient, and amazing"
— Jenny G. Perry.

"Once upon a time, Benjamin Franklin said, 'Some people die at twenty-five and aren't buried until they are seventy-five'..." Jimmy's dad began to read.

"What does he mean by that, dad?" 7-year-old Jimmy asked.

"Hmm... Good question. We may actually know

people who are dead at twenty-five, but dead in the sense that they have absolutely no zest for life, and they live like they have no purpose in this world whatsoever." Jimmy's dad replied, closing the book he was reading to Jimmy.

"How can you tell who they are?" Jimmy asked innocently.

"You can tell if you pay attention to how some people live, what they say, and what they do. And the idea here, Jimmy, is for you to learn from it."

"Ok, Dad, I get it. Tell me how to know these people."

"Growing up, I had an older cousin, Joe; he wasn't so much older than me. Joe usually waits for everyone to come and see him at home. He never goes to see anyone, unless someone specifically extends an invitation to him and picks him up. He is rarely happy, often grouchy, and he would only speak to you after you have initiated the contact."

"When you delve into Joe's everyday life by asking him questions like, 'how are you doing?' and 'what are you involved in?' His answers never vary. He responds to the first question with, 'I'm okay', or 'same old, same old'. To the second question, his *response echoes the same as the first with 'not much', or 'the usual'. Joe's usual response of 'okay' often seems to be saying that 'he is still in this world, but laughter, happiness, and enthusiasm for life forgot to call on him'. And his answer to the second question appears to indicate that nothing ever changes for him; the same old response means he is doing nothing that challenges him, inspires him, or contributes nothing to guide his steps forward. He lacked fervour for life, thus, achieved nothing, though educated. For most of us in the family, Joe was more dead than alive, he died a long time ago before he eventually died in 2016; he was only waiting to be buried."*

"It must be really sad to live that way, dad. I don't want to live like that when I grow up." Jimmy said, nodding with understanding.

"Yes, it is, and you don't have to wait till you grow up to not live like that, you can start now. However, there are many others, like Uncle Gabriel, Aunt Zinny, your older cousins - Kunle, Chinwe, and even your mom, who are all just the opposite of Joe. They are full of life; filled with anticipation in looking beyond the next horizon; filled with enthusiasm as they extend their warmth and compassion to everyone they meet or bubbling over with humour as they tackle both the hills and

valleys of life headlong. They never see a roadblock but only a solution; these are people who will give their services to others before thinking of their own needs. These are the people you 'want' to be around because it's impossible to stay moody and give up in their presence. They have an incredible zest for life."

This ushers in the leadership alphabet Z - Zest.

Every time I peel citrus fruits, especially oranges and tangerines, I love the natural zest flavour that sprinkles out of the peel. The sprinkle has a way of filling the air with a natural flavour. The Zest is energetic, fresh and promising. One of the reasons you cannot hide while taking an orange is that the zest will give you up.

Zest is defined as "living life with a sense of excitement, anticipation, and energy. Approaching life as an adventure, such that one has "motivation in challenging situations or tasks". Zest is essentially a concept of courage and involves acquiring the motivation to complete challenging situations and tasks. Those who have zest exude enthusiasm, excitement, and energy while approaching tasks in life. Hence, *"the concept of zest involves performing tasks wholeheartedly, while also being adventurous, vivacious and energetic."* (Positive Psychology, Wikipedia).

A lot of us hold off living life. We stop living in the present, and we draw up grand plans for a future yet to unveil. We neglect our present, and we deprive ourselves the serenity of watching the sunrise, the peace of watching the stars twinkle in the sky, the joy of watching the clouds gather storm. It is important to observe nature, breathe deep in and out, hug that child and be reminded of the innocence of childhood. Simply put, be present in your present!

In the words of Eleanor Roosevelt, *"the purpose of life is to live it, to taste the experience to the utmost, to reach out eagerly and without fear for a newer and richer experience."* Life is to be enjoyed; therefore, you need to live with zest. You cannot make the best out of life without zest. Your zeal to live must be intense. You must radiate positive energy, possibilities and love. Embrace life – laugh, love, dance, grow, share, be happy, observe the stars, stand in the rain, explore, read books, learn new skills. Keep growing, and approach living deliberately by making each day a masterpiece. To conquer life, you must carry in you a positive attitude. Let the zest for life consume you; be good and do good. Be adventurous – the greatest inventions are the product of an inquisitive mind. Ask questions.

Zest is contagious! When you exude energy and positivity, you begin to attract positive outcomes.

A zesty spirit is loved by many, and a zesty soul is rewarded by life. You are young and full of energy, do not let anything take your enthusiasm from you. You will come across people and situations that will attempt to kill your optimism and extinguish your zeal, but always remember; 'You are a force for good'. Your validations and happiness must derive from you, not from others else they take it away.

You are indeed special, and I celebrate you! I dedicate the lines below to a greater you:

> *I wish you would;*
> *Dance with the wind, Shine with the sun*
> *Twinkle with the stars, Pour like the rain*
> *Grow with the moon, Laugh with the thunder*
> *Be grateful for your breath.*
> *Enjoy life and embrace living*
> *Be full of Zest until you go to rest.*
>
> -Odunayo Sanya

Exercise:

a) Why is zest so important in life?

b) What would you do differently to show more zest for life? Make a list of what you can do.

WORKBOOK

www.ingramcontent.com/pod-product-compliance
Lightning Source LLC
Chambersburg PA
CBHW071305110426
42743CB00042B/1178